Beside

Quiet Waters

Beside
Quiet Waters

· · · · ·

REFLECTIONS

ON THE PSALMS

IN OUR

EVERYDAY LIVES

James D. Capozzi, M.D.

CONTINUUM · NEW YORK

HOUSTON PUBLIC LIBRARY

R01120 77725

1999

The Continuum Publishing Company
370 Lexington Avenue, New York, N.Y. 10017

Copyright © 1999 by James D. Capozzi

All rights reserved. No part of this book may be
reproduced, stored in a retrieval system, or
transmitted, in any form or by any means, electronic,
mechanical, photocopying, recording, or otherwise,
without the written permission of
The Continuum Publishing Company.

Printed in the United States of America

Library of Congress Cataloging-in-Publication Data

Capozzi, James D.
Beside quiet waters : reflections on the psalms in
our everyday lives / James D. Capozzi.
p.   cm.
Includes bibliographical references.
ISBN 0-8264-1145-2
1. Bible. O.T. Psalms—Meditations.   I. Title.
BS1430.4.C36   1999
242'.5—dc21   98-55720
CIP

Scripture taken from The Holy Bible,
New International Version.
Copyright © 1973, 1978, 1984 International Bible Society.
Used by permission of Zondervan Bible Publishers.

To my wife, Kathie,
who has been by my side always,
for encouraging me to write
when I really did not think I could
and
to my daughters, Kristen,
Alaina, and Nicole,
who in addition to providing me
with an endless source of material,
have given me a glimpse
of heaven here on earth.

Acknowledgment

God said, "Let there be light," and there was light. He said, "Let there be an expanse between the waters, let the land produce vegetation, let the water teem with living creatures," and it was so. It is obvious, from all published accounts, that the Lord worked alone on these projects. The creation of *Beside Quiet Waters*, on the other hand, was far from a solitary effort. Many people helped me in the formation of this book, some directly, some indirectly, but all by the influence they have had on my life.

To my family, not just the mommy and three young women I live with, but my entire family for their support, their stories, their experiences, and their love. Without those things, I would not have grown in my faith .

To all of my friends and family who have left us here and are now with the Lord. Even from afar you continue to inspire and support me.

To Cindy Scavelli, my friend, neighbor, and personal editor, without your comments and corrections this manuscript would never have made it past the publisher's discard pile.

To Andrea Waldron, for handing me *Voices of Silence*, the book that started the whole process going.

To Ralph Zeuthen, writer, patient, friend, for suggesting that I change the title of this book from something very ordinary to something quietly captivating and for all of your other suggestions.

To Frank Oveis and Continuum, for giving an unknown author a chance to share his reflections.

To the Rev. Philip Eichner, past president of Chaminade High School and current president of Kellenberg Memorial High School, for guiding me in my faith and my introspection. You have taught me that the journey is just as important as the destination.

To Ephraim Rubenstein, the most talented artist, the most gifted intellect, and the most enjoyable old goat a person could ever know. Your art work is unquestionably a gift from the Lord, your friendship, a gift from the heart.

To all of my friends and family who helped me grow, learn, reflect, and yes, even write. You were there always when I had questions and doubts. You were there when I needed someone to bounce ideas off of, someone to encourage me to keep going, someone to say, "Hey, these are nice, keep writing."

To the Lord, for providing me with the gift of words and the insights on which to base those words. I pray that this book will bring even one reader closer to your love.

Thank you all.

Preface

The reflections that you are about to read are taken from everyday life. I am neither a theologian nor priest, biblical scholar nor divinity student. I have no particular religious scholarly training other than parochial grammar and high school. What I am though is son, husband, father, physician, teacher, writer, neighbor, carpenter, garbage-taker-outer, dog walker, gardener, and sometime house painter. I wrote these reflections based upon all of those things, that all of us do, each and every day.

So what right do I have to comment on the Psalms? The very same right that each of you have. The Bible, I believe, was written by divine inspiration, to explore God's relationship to us and with us. It is a book, or more correctly, a collection of books, in which God is revealed to us. The writings teach us about our creator and about our relationship to that creator and to each other.

To be quite honest, until recently, I had very little interest in the Psalms. On the several occasions, when I set out to read the Bible cover to cover, it was always the Book of Psalms that I would gloss over. What could I learn from this collection of four thousand year old poems? What I did glean from them meant little to me. Without Babylonian neighbors to smite, jaw bones to break, or family lineage to curse, what could I have in common with these lyrics?

Then all of that changed. A fellow churchgoer recommended to me Frank Bianco's *Voices of Silence*. She thought I would find it interesting reading. Following several personal tragedies, including the death of his teenage son, Mr. Bianco was searching for an inner peace. He recalled feeling a sense of tranquility in the past when he had attended a service at a Trappist monastery. *Voices of Silence* explores his attempt to recapture that inner peace by living at the Trappist Abbey of Gethsemani in Kentucky.

The Trappist monks chant the Psalms several times throughout the day. They have done so for hundreds of years in all of their abbeys throughout the world. In fact, all other activities and obligations take a back seat to these prayer services.

Now I was baffled. What did these monks, some of them among the brightest theologians, thinkers, and philosophers of the church, see in these Psalms? What was it in these poems that made people stop whatever they were doing, several times a day, to recite them?

Mr. Bianco, too, sought an explanation. He came to learn that the Psalms contain the entire gamut of human conditions. Their words can be harsh. Many of them contain strong language. It takes courage and honesty to read them.

As Father Matthew Kelty points out in his book *Sermons in a Monastery:*

> People do not know and do not want to know themselves. They much prefer to live on a frag-

ile surface....Hand such people a Psalter and they will be ill at ease with anything except the pretty ones about the glory of God and the beauty of nature. But turn to some of the wilder psalms and they will find the words inappropriate and the sentiments unchristian. As undoubtedly they are. But until you have penetrated with Christ into your own depth, much of you is also unchristian and will remain so. The psalms can teach us much of this, of the conflict with evil within us. Bring us face to face with the traitor in our own heart: the two timer, the time server, the false friend. Who has not met the demon of envy, of jealousy, of greed, of hatred, lurking in the dark shadows of his depth.

So there it was. The gauntlet had been thrown. Did I have the courage now to read the Psalms with all of this in mind, to look into my own heart, my own experiences and find that gamut of human conditions of which the psalmist wrote? These are not poems about a small desert nation from another millenium. They are about me. They are about my hatred, my greed, my envy, my guilt. And if that is true, then I need to explore those sentiments in the things I do and see everyday.

I invite you, then, to join me on this journey. As Father Kelty points out, it may not be a pleasant trip. We may not like what we see in ourselves along the way. We may not want to see. But I assure you, the trip will be worth it.

Please note that there is plenty of room in the margins of each reflection to write your own thoughts and experiences. Use this book. Mark it. Interact with it. My daughters often chide me that I don't know how to read without a pencil in my hand. I encourage you to pick up my bad habit. I look forward to hearing your comments and reading your own reflections on those passages that have particularly affected your life.

In peace,
J.D.C.

Blessed is the man who does not walk in the counsel of the wicked or stand in the way of sinners or sit in the seat of mockers. But his delight is in the law of the Lord.
Psalm 1:1–2

How stupid I feel when I do the wrong thing, when I try to get away with things that I know are wrong, when I mock people behind their backs, when my thoughts should be wholesome and pure but instead are wicked and vengeful.

I never feel good when I've chosen evil over good, wrong over right. It's quite the opposite feeling when I know I've done the right thing, even if this may have been the harder road to travel.

Robert Frost spoke of that road so eloquently in his poetry. That is the road the Lord has asked us to travel, not the path of the wicked but the more difficult path of righteousness and truth, not the easy road but truly the road less traveled.

Lord, watch over me. Guide me to this path of righteousness.

✣

Do I often take the easier course even if I know it is not always for the best?

The One enthroned in heaven laughs, the Lord scoffs at them.

Psalm 2:4

Have you ever sat unnoticed and watched children play? Their games, their discussions, their interactions can be fascinating. Whether they are playing house or war, they have a definite protocol that must be followed. They have established very specific rules of play to which each of the participants must adhere, or suffer the consequences. Many an argument will ensue over the slightest breech of protocol.

As the outside observer, I can understand the importance of these rules. But I can also see how they can be given too much emphasis. I often find myself mediating fights, saying, "Oh, what's the difference if she has two blue ones or three, or whether he took three swings or four?" Kids can get so caught up in the things that we see as being so petty.

Can't they see how unimportant these trivialities are? Can't we? Are we not exactly the same? I often get myself so worked-up, so bent out of shape, over things that are so insignificant. Then I stop and picture the Lord sitting up there laughing at me.

I'm caught up in my own little pettiness and He's probably shaking his head saying, "After all I've taught you, haven't you learned anything? You still don't know what's important in life?"

Lord, I'll try not to be so petty if you'll try not to laugh so hard.

❈

Do I mix up my priorites thinking the petty things in life are important?

O Lord, how many are my foes! How many rise up against me! But you are a shield around me, O Lord.

Psalm 3:1, 3

So often we are threatened by our foes, in the workplace, in our neighborhoods, in business. They seem eager to threaten our lives, our families, our relationships, even our faith. They would love to see us fail in any of our endeavors.

If we acknowledge their actions, we empower them. If we fight against them, we have stooped to their level and have therefore already lost.

We can struggle with them, or we can ask the Lord to be our shield. Alone I may feel powerless but with my Lord I am His protected.

✠

Do I find myself reacting to those trying to persecute me instead of acting with the Lord's protection?

Answer me when I call to you, O my righteous God.
Give me relief from my distress; be merciful and hear my
prayer. Let the light of your face shine upon us, O Lord.
You have filled my heart with greater joy.

Psalm 4:1, 6–7

How often I turn to the Lord when disaster strikes. Whether it's a true catastrophe, a major illness or the death of a loved one, or the simple mishaps of daily life, I know He will guide me and give me comfort.

And in the good times, I confess, I wander and seek out delusions and false gods: prestige, money, power, possessions. They seem so tempting when times are good, but their comfort is temporary and shallow.

So I call to the Lord to hear my prayer, to receive my burden, to bring me peace. I ask Him to shine his face on me and show me the real good.

He allows us to ask Him and I have asked often. He has indeed filled my heart with the greater joy. I have tried to make room for Him in my silence, to listen for His divine guidance in my heart.

I have turned to the Lord and now I can truly sleep in peace.

✠

Do I only come to the Lord with my problems and
turn away from Him during the good times?

Not a word from their mouth can be trusted; their heart is filled with destruction.

Psalm 5:9

A colleague of mine was recently in a business arrangement with associates who would not have hesitated to hasten his financial or professional demise. Monies were misappropriated, clients were steered away. There was a definite jealousy about any of his successes.

He often thought about seeking revenge but in his heart, he knew it was wrong. So he sought refuge in the Lord. Just as the psalmist had done thousands of years ago, he prayed for the Lord's protection.

Almost without warning, the Lord made straight a path before him. Several other practice opportunities became available. He left that original group and it collapsed soon afterwards.

There is no doubt in my mind that the Lord delivered him from his enemies. He cleared a path for him and protected him. The Lord truly surrounded him with His favors.

Do I trust the Lord enough to follow His ways or do I resist them in favor of my own agenda?

O Lord, do not rebuke me in your anger or discipline me in your wrath. Be merciful to me, O Lord.

Psalm 6:1

How many of us, as parents, can learn from the psalmist's plea to the Father? It is so easy in our anger, our frustration, and our haste, to yell and scream and punish. But what comes of it? Our children are hurt or frightened. They themselves may become angry and spiteful. And worst of all, we always hate ourselves afterwards for the way we behaved.

I hate yelling at my kids. I hate the way it makes them feel. I hate the way I look in my anger. I hate the way I must sound to them. Most importantly, I hate the lesson I'm teaching. It is certainly not a lesson of love, kindness, patience, and understanding.

We have all prayed to the Lord to forgive us, to be merciful, to forget our own indiscretions. Shouldn't we be that understanding with our children? Without a doubt, they need our discipline but not suffused with anger and wrath. My children can only learn to be understanding and merciful if that is the example I set for them.

✠

Am I as understanding with those who anger me,
as I ask the Lord to be with me?

If I have done evil to him who is at peace with me . . .

Psalm 7:4

It is a known fact that abused children will often falsely accuse a well liked teacher or authority figure of the atrocities inflicted upon them. The theory is that the child fears no punishment from the individual who has been so caring towards them. Of course, these accusations are devastating to innocent adults, their careers, and their families.

On a more personal level, I know I have often come home from work defeated and crushed. I am unable to lash out at the real offenders, so my wife and my children take the brunt of my anger and frustration.

Likewise, the newspapers are filled with stories of do-gooders, Samaritans, who have been set upon by those to whom they were so generous. People who've opened their hearts, homes, families, and purses, only to be robbed, betrayed, beaten, and even murdered.

Only by attacking those who are truly at peace with me can I demonstrate the true depths to which I can sink.

※

How often have I betrayed the trust of those who have opened themselves completely to me?

O Lord, our Lord, how majestic is your name in all the earth! You have set your glory above the heavens. When I consider your heavens, the work of your fingers, the moon and the stars, which you have set in place, what is man that you are mindful of him, the son of man that you care for him?

Psalm 8:1–4

Have you ever stood in an open field on a clear, crisp night and looked skyward? The vast beauty of the universe is so apparent. The stars stretch across the sky to infinity. You try to pick out some recognizable constellation in an attempt to organize a vastness that our minds can barely comprehend. In the midst of this infinite expanse, we realize that we are little more than a speck. We are completely and utterly insignificant when compared to this enormousness.

Yet the Lord tells us otherwise. In His eyes, we are everything. The Lord created us in His image, in His likeness. He chose us to watch over all of His creation. He sanctifies, protects, guides and loves everyone of us.

To the small child, the world must seem infinite. Even within their own family, they may often seem insignificant. But to their parents, they are everything. Parents' lives revolve around their children's safety, their growth, their education, their love. It is inconceivable to them that their children could be forgotten. Do you think it is any different with our Lord?

⌖

Do we realize the special place the Lord has given us within His magnificent creation?

I will praise you, O Lord, with all my heart; I will tell of all your wonders. I will be glad and rejoice in you; I will sing praise to your name, O Most High.

Psalm 9:1–2

Not many of us sing praises any longer. Oh, we may mumble through the words. We begrudgingly mouth along, but we don't often sing praises to the Lord. The choir and cantor sing praises. They sing their hearts out. We lip sync.

Young people rarely sing. Teenagers never sing praises to God's name, not in church anyway. At a certain age, it's not very cool to sing in public. Not only don't they sing, but their feelings about their parents' singing are quite apparent.

When she was younger, my middle daughter sang praises in church without reservation. Unfortunately, every praise she sang, began with, "Somewhere, over the rainbow, way up high." Surrounding churchgoers were moved to laughter.

I guess the best advice I've heard, with regards to singing praises to the Lord's name, came from a priest who goaded his parishoners into song by advising them, "If you've been blessed with a good voice, this is your chance to thank the Lord; and if you've been given a terrible voice, well then, this is your chance to get back at Him." So whether it's payback or performance, let's sing our hearts out.

✠

Can I abandon my inhibitions about singing and praise God's name in song?

Why, O Lord, do you stand far off? Why do you hide yourself in times of trouble?

Psalm 10:1

The other day I was in a bookstore shopping with my seven-year-old daughter. I had been browsing in one particular section. She was ricocheting from aisle to aisle throughout the store. At one point, she lost her bearings and couldn't find me even though I had not moved. I heard her calling out to me. I returned the call. When she found me, she said, "Why did you move without telling me? I couldn't find you." I explained to her I had not moved.

My guess is that we do the same thing with the Lord. At times, He seems far off, even hidden. But in reality, He hasn't moved. It is we who become distracted and lost. It is we who lose sight of the Lord in pursuit of other things. Thankfully, He calls out to us so that we may reorient ourselves and find the Lord, where He has always been.

❊

Do I lose sight of the Lord in pursuit
of my own distractions?

For look, the wicked bend their bows; they set their arrows against the strings to shoot from the shadows at the upright in heart. When the foundations are being destroyed, what can the righteous do?

Psalm 11:2–3

It is difficult to turn on the news or read the newspaper today without some sense that the basic foundation of our society, of humankind, is being destroyed. The very fabric of our society is being torn to shreds. Husbands killing wives, parents abusing infants, judges breaking laws, priests molesting children. Heinous and horrific crimes are being committed. These are crimes that undermine even our most basic and primitive sense of morality. These truly are arrows shot from the shadows.

But should the righteous turn and fire? Or should we head for the mountains and abandon the farm? No, that is not the answer, nor has it ever been. For if we truly believe in the Lord, then we must take refuge in Him. The righteous must stand their ground. The fabric must be resewn. The foundation rebuilt.

Robert Fulghum, in his wonderful book *All I Really Need to Know I Learned in Kindergarten*, talks about those simple principles of human kindness that we all learned in childhood: sharing, playing fair, cleaning up, holding hands. Maybe then, if we take hold of the Lord's hand, and start with these simple blocks, we can begin to rebuild this crumbling foundation.

Do I do all that I can to rebuild the foundation or do I just assist in its destruction?

Help, Lord, for the godly are no more; the faithful have vanished from among men. Everyone lies to his neighbor; their flattering lips speak with deception.

Psalm 12:1–2

There is so much talk about our society entering the information highway. Never before in the history of civilization has so much information been available to so many, at the click of a mouse. But amid this wealth of information, we are so much a society surrounded by lies and liars.

We are surrounded by information yet truthfulness is scarce. We lie. We lie to each other; we lie on applications; we lie on tests; we lie on taxes. We even lie to ourselves. In fact, lying has become an accepted part of our lives. Politicians lie; we expect it. Manufacturers lie; we are not surprised.

We seem to have entered a time when dishonesty has become the norm. The person who tells the truth, who comes clean, who doesn't try to get away with something, is laughed at. He or she is the fool.

And yet, honesty is so refreshing. We have all felt its effects. We have all had that wonderful feeling of shedding the lies and coming clean. Let us pray, as individuals and as a society, to strive for that feeling more often. Honesty is, unquestionably, the harder course but the one with the greater reward in the end.

⌗

Has lying become an integral part of my life and honesty the rarity?

How long must I wrestle with my thoughts and every day have sorrow in my heart?

Psalm 13:2

There was a television commercial several years ago showing a football coach explaining some intricate play to his team. In the middle of his explanation, one of the players said, "But coach, I thought I was supposed to go this way." The coach replied, "Don't think, Tucker, just block."

I once had a golf pro tell me the same thing. "You think too much. Don't think. Just swing."

Think too much. I never thought that was possible, to think too much. I always thought that thinking was a good thing. But I guess, like anything else, too much of a good thing can be bad for us. We can sometimes become so engrossed in our thoughts that we become paralyzed in our actions.

Thinking is great and, obviously, essential to our existence. But sometimes, we just have to follow our hearts. As we have all discovered, many things are beyond our comprehension anyway. Things like human suffering, who we fall in love with, and even God's very existence, defy logical thought. St. Thomas Aquinas speaks of God's existence in terms of "to know God as unknowable."

So instead of tormenting ourselves with thinking and overthinking, let's just go with our hearts. Swing away! I think we'll hit the ball better anyway.

⌗

Do I find myself paralyzed in thought and unable to act?

*The Lord looks down from heaven on the sons of men to
see if there are any who understand, any who seek God.*
Psalm 14:2

Several years ago my church held a spiritual retreat.
The retreat ran for five consecutive evenings for about
two hours each night. A visiting Paulist priest was the
speaker. On the first evening, the church was about
half filled. By the third evening, it was completely
filled. By the fourth, there was standing room only. The
priest voiced his amazement at the growing crowd. He
pointed out that this was a very special community
where, no doubt, the Holy Spirit was at work.

But he also took that opportunity to point out this
generation's disenchantment with life. We are obviously not satisfied with faster cars, bigger houses, and
more toys. Many of us have experienced the empty and
fleeting happiness of more and better possessions. Undoubtedly our quest for happinesss is not found in
what we buy. Our emptiness is not filled with credit
card receipts. We all know there is more to living than
all of that.

So let us continue to search for the Lord. Let us
strive to understand Him. Then when He looks down
from heaven, He will find those at least trying to understand and indeed, seeking the Lord.

⌖

*Am I actively seeking the Lord, or are my
possessions all that I need?*

Lord, who may dwell in your sanctuary? Who may live on your holy hill? He whose walk is blameless and who does what is righteous, who speaks the truth from his heart and has no slander on his tongue, who does his neighbor no wrong and who casts no slur on his fellow-man.

Psalm 15:1–3

My youngest daughter is three years old. I often watch her behavior in utter amazement. Her actions are fascinating. At this young age, she truly embodies those virtues that the psalmist extols.

At three years old, her walk is blameless. I rarely, if ever, see her doing what is not righteous. She doesn't cheat or steal or sneak. Without question, she speaks the truth from her heart. Sometimes so much truth, that we, her parents, cringe at her blatant honesty. She doesn't speak ill of her friends. And the behavior of which I am most proud is her unquestioning generosity. She will share her toys, her food, even her candy, without hesitation.

So of whom is the psalmist speaking, the righteous person seeking God or the three-year-old child? Or are they really one and the same? No wonder Jesus instructed us to become like little children. I can learn a lot from my kids, maybe even the pathway to the Lord's sanctuary.

❖

*Will I be asked to dwell in the Lord's sanctuary
or live on His holy hill?*

Lord, you have assigned me my portion and my cup.
Psalm 16:5

I spoke to a patient today, a young man with severe arthritis of his hips. I offered him help in the way of joint replacement surgery. He wanted the surgery but was not planning to comply with the postoperative restrictions. He was not hoping for a full, unrestricted lifestyle. He was demanding it. I told him that would not be possible after this type of surgery. He refused to accept his medical condition. Consequently, he refused to adjust his lifestyle to benefit from what could have been highly successful surgery. He refused to accept his portion and his cup.

Many a mystic has told us that all is right with the world. It is we who are screwing things up. The problem is not with the world. The problem is not out there. Rather, the problem is with us fighting the reality. We try to make what is into what we think it should be.

Life is going to take its course. We can try and change the direction of the river but we'll only end up all wet. We can spend the rest of our lives reacting to every perceived stone in our path or we can accept what is and go on from there. But to let go, to truly let go, requires that we put our faith in the Lord. We must believe that He has assigned us our portion and our cup.

Am I able to resist trying to change reality because it doesn't fit my notion of how things should be?

They close up their callous hearts and their mouths speak with arrogance.

Psalm 17:10

During my preadolescent years, I was an altar boy at our church. Before a Sunday afternoon wedding ceremony, an elderly woman came to the back of the church to ask the priest if there was a Mass that afternoon. He replied that there wasn't; there was only a wedding ceremony. She asked if he knew where there might be a late afternoon Sunday Mass. He begrudgingly told her the name of a nearby parish with evening services. She asked if he knew how to get there or if she could get a cab. Her told her to try the bus. He couldn't call a cab for her.

The bus stop was a good four or five blocks away. Buses run very sporadically in the suburbs. It could be hours before a bus came.

There was a phone in the sacristy that called into the rectory. One call to the rectory and the receptionist could have called for a cab. This was an elderly woman trying to get to church. Even if he couldn't get her a cab, a kind word would have gone a long way in comforting this woman.

I remember being so angry at the priest. That was one of my first experiences with a truly callous heart. I could not believe the priest's lack of compassion for this elderly woman and her simple request for an evening Mass.

I guess we should indeed be fearful of the enemy with the callous heart and the arrogant mouth, for it may be us.

❦

How many times have I turned down someone's simple request for a little assistance because I just didn't feel like helping?

You save the humble but bring low those whose eyes are haughty.

Psalm 18:27

There is a story from ancient Greek mythology in which all of the heroes from past epics are taken to a room in the afterlife. In this room, they are allowed to choose a new life. The story progresses with all of the famous warrriors and heroes choosing lives of fame and fortune. They choose to become kings and queens, noblemen, athletes, and celebrities. They choose from among the most prestigious and glorious.

Odysseus, the hero of Homer's epic poem *The Odyssey,* is probably the most famous of all of those allowed to choose. He chooses last. As the author of this story so eloquently describes, Odysseus searches for his choice throughout the room and, in a darkened corner, finds the tattered, dust-covered life of the humble man. Odysseus takes this one as his own.

Here, in this writing from the ancient Greeks, the most powerful and famous of all of the warriors sees the greatest honor in a life of humility. He could have chosen of any life, any fame, any wealth. He chose humility.

How often do we live our lives in search of fame, fortune, and prestige? The true honor, though, is in the life of the humble servant.

✠

Are we not more inspired when our heroes of today are humble individuals rather than arrogant braggarts?

The heavens declare the glory of God; the skies proclaim the work of his hands.

Psalm 19:1

Several years ago we celebrated my wife's parents' 45th wedding anniversary. Since they both had some significant health problems, there was some fear that they might not see fifty years together (which, by the way, they both did). So we had a huge 45th party.

The party was very exciting. It took weeks of planning, arranging and purchasing. There were clandestine meetings, cooking at one sister's house or another. Cryptic phone conversations relayed back and forth. Few military operations are carried out with such covertness.

The day of the party finally arrived. It was to be an outdoor party. There was a dance floor, DJ, pool, buffet area, and umbrella-covered tables. Miraculously, the weather was perfect. Scores of cars arrived. Somehow they went unnoticed, even on a small cul-de-sac. The food was plentiful. The guests partied. My in-laws were completely and utterly surprised.

The day could not have been more perfect. The celebration lasted well into the morning hours. The following day the family returned for clean-up detail, leftovers, and reminiscing.

As we all drove away, late that afternoon, a gentle rain began to fall. A beautiful rainbow arched across the sky directly over the house where our family had been gathered for the past two days.

There was no doubt in my mind, no doubt in the minds of all of us in that car, that that sky was proclaiming the glory of God. The past two days could not have gone more perfectly and that rainbow in the heavens was just one more sign that the Lord had blessed that entire weekend.

Do I appreciate nature's celebration of God's glory and honor?

May he give you the desire of your heart and make all your plans succeed. We will shout for joy when you are victorious and will lift up our banners in the name of our God. Some trust in chariots and some in horses, but we trust in the name of the Lord our God.

Psalm 20:4–5, 7

During a period late in my orthopedic training, I was having a difficult time with my board exams. I turned to a book on prayer to help me through. There were two interesting points that the author had made. The first was the recommendation that all of our prayers should begin with the words, "If it is your will, Lord." Jesus also taught us to pray this way in the Lord's Prayer, "thy will be done."

The second point that the author made was that we must be careful for what we pray because we may indeed get it. In other words, we might pray for things that we think are best for us, but in reality, may make our lives much more burdensome.

The psalmist speaks of God granting the desires of our heart. He doesn't say our heads, our wallets, or our groins. The world is filled with hundreds of unhappy Lotto winners, rich people, now miserable in their newfound wealth. There are thousands of unhappy relationships between two people who may have had little more than an initial physical attraction to one another. Faster cars, more money, fancier clothes, better jewelry, we've all had these desires. But what are the desires of our hearts? Do we put our trust in chariots and horses, or in the name of the Lord our God?

❖

Do I pray to the Lord with my heart or merely to expand my wallet, cupboard, and garage?

He asked you for life, and you gave it to him.

Psalm 21:4

Every once in a while a line from the Psalms jumps out as being so poignant, so beautiful, so profound, that it just grabs at your heart. Such is this line from the Twenty-first Psalm. It is such a simple phrase, no word even longer than two syllables. Yet it can hold for us meaning on a multitude of levels.

He asked you for life and you gave it to him. Is this a description of the creation account, with God breathing life into Adam? Or is it the story of Lazarus being raised from the dead? Or Jesus rising up on the third day?

Or is it the newly wed couple, choosing to answer the call within their marriage, to procreate and take their relationship to that next higher plane of family?

Or does that single line reflect the choice of the unwed mother, who decides to keep the life alive within her, rather than abort his or her very existence?

Or is the psalmist describing one of the most selfless acts we will ever witness, the nurturing mother answering her child's cries of hunger, suckling at her breasts, literally giving him life from life?

Or is it, on a more personal level, the story of our own spritual life? The story of our dying to the secular world and rising to a new life in the Holy Spirit?

After all, it's just one simple sentence.

❈

Do I do all that I can to encourage life, whether it be emotional, physical, or spiritual?

In you our fathers put their trust; they trusted and you delivered them. They cried to you and were saved; in you they trusted and were not disappointed.

Psalm 22:4–5

It strikes me so odd, at times, that our nation, the United States of America, was built on the basic premise of a belief in God. Our forefathers were spiritual men. Their belief in God is evident in our Declaration of Independence and in our Constitution. Our patriotic songs ask for God's blessing and protection. Our armed forces continue to serve under the sentiment of God and country. Even our money says that we, as Americans, put our faith in God.

Our forefathers, in their wisdom, saw firsthand the conflicts that could arise when church and government become entwined. So they asked, even legislated, that the two remain separate.

But separation is not denial. Separation is not rejection. Separation is not abjuration. Separation does not mean no mention of God in our schools, or no acknowledgment of the divine creation of humankind. It has gone as far as court battles over Christmas lights on municipal buildings.

Is this really what our founding fathers had in mind? Has separation become synonymous with elimination? Is God an integral part of our nation's existence or do we need to print new money?

✺

Have I compartmentalized my life into religious and secular, or is God an integral part of all my affairs?

He makes me lie down in green pastures, he leads me be-side quiet waters, he restores my soul.

Psalm 23:2

This psalm is so rich in imagery that it is difficult to choose one line on which to reflect. Every verse raises up images worthy of contemplation and reflection. Every line conjures up feelings of calm and tranquility.

During my thirteenth summer, I went to a Boy Scout camp in upstate New York for several weeks. It was a period of tremendous activity and growth: physical activity, mental skills, social development, sexual information (or misinformation), bravado, comraderie, and challenges. The two weeks were an avalanche of mental and physical growth. It was exhilarating. It was draining.

During that time, several of us from my troop discovered a small island tucked away deep in the forest. It was set in the middle of a slow-moving brook. The island was only about eight feet across. There were two or three pine trees and soft needle ground cover. A narrow, single, felled tree trunk served as the only connection between the island and the riverbank.

I would go to that island often. I usually sought its comfort and solitude late in the afternoon, just before dinner. I would sit alone or with a friend in quiet rest and meditation. The gentle babbling brook, the silent movement of the trout, the motionless pines, and the dense surrounding forest, all served to soothe and restore my soul. Even the adolescent soul was not beyond restoration.

✠

Do I allow the Lord to soothe and restore me, o
am I always moving at breakneck speed?

He who has clean hands and a pure heart, who ==does not lift up his soul to an idol or swear by what is false. He will receive blessings from the Lord and vindication from God his Savior. Such is the generation of those who seek him.

Psalm 24:4–6

Clean hands, a pure heart, worships no idol, does not swear to what is false, that is the generation that seeks the Lord. Are we that generation?

I was reflecting recently on my generation, where it had begun and where it was going. It began with the loftiest ideals. Ending an unjust war. Peace. Love. Brotherhood and sisterhood. Sharing. Acceptance. Communes. "Hey man, live and let live." It was a generation that should have changed everything. It was a generation that spoke of universal brotherhood, universal acceptance, universal love.

But what happened? What changed? I look around at our society today and those exalted ideals are all but gone. Brotherhood, sharing, acceptance—nonexistent. Peace, openess, love—gone. We are surrounded on every continent by wars of hatred: ethnic wars, racial wars, sexual wars, economic wars, and religious wars. Our hearts have turned inward, our possessions worshiped. Swearing to what is false has become the norm. Our hands are filthy with greed, deceit, dishonesty, lust, immorality, and pride.

Are we the generation that seeks the Lord? I think

we were. I think we might have been. I think we may have lost our way.

✠

Have I abandoned those ideals of my youth for false idols, soiled hands, and an impure heart?

Remember not the sins of my youth and my rebellious ways; according to your love remember me, for you are good, O Lord.

Psalm 25:7

The sins of my youth. Is it just me or does everyone look back at some of the more inane moments of youth and say, "What was I thinking? Was I really that _____!" Supply any appropriate adjective: stupid, young, foolish, immature, self-centered. But who among us wasn't?

We were all young, foolish and rebellious.

When I think of some of the risks I took, I am amazed that I didn't fall into harm's way more often than I did. And, as the psalmist suggests, who wouldn't like to have the sins of our youth forgotten, all of those mistakes erased?

Yet, those sins, those risks, those rebellions are all a part of who we are. They are an integral part of our growth. You can't mature into an adult without the painful forgings of youth.

As parents, we, hopefully, understand that. I expect my children to make their share of mistakes. I can't prevent that. Nor should I. That's part of growing up. If I'm lucky, I can prevent the truly dangerous ones from injuring them. Hopefully, they can learn and grow from the others. But I must look at all of their mistakes with tenderness, love, and understanding, as hopefully they will with mine. If we can do that with our own children, don't you think the Father will do the same with us?

·✠·

Have I grown from the sins of my youth or are they just painful reminders of my immaturity?

I love the house where you live, O Lord, the place where your glory dwells.

Psalm 26:8

As part of their preparation for marriage the Catholic Church requires engaged couples to attend pre-Cana conferences. My wife and I are one of the married couple instructors for our church's pre-Cana program. One of the evening's topics is spirituality.

As an exercise prior to the discussion, we ask the married couples to build their ideal church. On index cards, they write several qualities or ideals they would want as the foundation for their new church. The group then begins a discussion to choose the six most important building blocks. Duplicate cards are discarded and similar concepts combined until they arrive at their ideal church. Their building blocks usually consist of ideals such as honesty, acceptance, faith, kindness, forgiveness, love. We ask the couples to compare their own real churches to the one they've built.

We then ask them, more importantly we think, how does their relationship compare to this ideal church? Does their marriage contain these same qualities that they found so important in the church?

Families are now being referred to as domestic churches. I don't think the phrase is simply a euphemism. Our families are the basis of our faith in the Lord. Our families are the places where most of us first learned the beliefs we hold, the spirituality we embody.

Our families, our homes, our domestic churches are the places where the Lord's glory dwells.

✠

Am I doing all that I can to make my home a domestic church where my family's faith can nurture and grow?

Hear my voice when I call, O Lord: be merciful to me and answer me.

Psalm 27:7

Undoubtedly, one of the most frightening experiences for anyone is to be lost. I remember, as a youngster, "losing" my mom countless times in department stores. She would often be no more than a clothes rack away but to a young child that distance was enormous.

Yet, just the sound of her voice was enough to allay my fears. I didn't need to see her. I just needed to know she was there. I see this with my own children. There is that periodic verbal check-in whenever we are shopping.

So isn't it natural that we, God's children, would do the same with our Father in heaven? We're not asking that He condone our every action or grant our every request. Just that He be merciful and periodically answer our call. The sound of His voice is enough to reassure us that we have not lost our way.

❖

Where have I heard the Lord's voice in my own life?

Do not drag me away with the wicked, with those who do evil, who speak cordially with their neighbors but harbor malice in their hearts.

Psalm 28:3

It has become all too common to read about the atrocities citizens of warring nations inflict upon one another, not that war crimes have ever been a rarity. What has become all too familiar, though, is not only the brutality of these crimes but the fact that they are being committed by citizens of the same country. These are often civil wars, pitting citizen against citizen, neighbor against neighbor.

I am astounded at the sight of neighbors beating, torturing, murdering, the very people who previously lived next door to them. I recently read an article about the Bosnian conflict. A man was tortured, castrated, and left to bleed to death by the very same person he lunched with in high school. From lunch mate to murderer, what happened?

But don't we do the same thing in a much less barbaric, yet just as effective way? A cordial wave from the front door while harboring feelings of ill will. A nod hello across the azaleas while speaking ill behind their backs. Neighborly chatting at the grocery store yet feeling jealous of their successes. It is not the physical violence of war-torn nations but the sentiments can be oh so similar.

❧

Have I truly succeeded in loving my neighbor as myself?

The voice of the Lord is over the waters....The voice of the Lord is powerful; the voice of the Lord is majestic. The voice of the Lord breaks cedars....The voice of the Lord strikes with flashes of lightning. The voice of the Lord shakes the desert....The voice of the Lord twists the oaks and strips the forest bare.

Psalm 29:3–9

Of all of the images we have of our Lord, an auditory image is probably not one of them. We have seen countless paintings and artist's renditions. We can all conjur up some mental image of our Lord in our mind's eye.

But none of us, I believe, has ever heard the Lord's voice. We have read numerous accounts of the Lord speaking to people but we have personally never heard Him speak. No tapes exist. There are no lost recordings to be discovered. There is no soundtrack to go along with the book.

Yet the psalmist has chosen the image of the Lord's voice to convey his message. A voice that can shake deserts, twist oak trees, reign over the seas...and we have not heard it? Or have we?

Is it that same voice of the elderly lady you helped with her packages and she thanked you? Or the close friend you supported through his recent family crisis? Or the small child who puts her arms around your neck and says, "Daddy, I love you."

For those voices, too, can move mountains. Those spoken acts of kindness can also come like flashes of lightning. So maybe I have heard the Lord's voice but I just didn't recognize it.

❉

Have we been careful enough to listen for the Lord's voice in those places where we least expect to find Him?

For his anger lasts only a moment, but his favor lasts a lifetime; weeping may remain for a night, but rejoicing comes in the morning.

Psalm 30:5

I am amazed at how quickly one's life can change. Literally, within seconds, a whole life can be turned around. A sudden car accident, an unexpected injury, a catastrophic illness. These can occur almost instantaneously and yet can change our lives forever.

Likewise, our weeping can be turned into joy in those same few seconds. A biopsy report that comes back negative, an unexpected call with a new job offer, the birth of a newborn child. Situations that seem hopeless can become, in an instant, cause for celebration.

I can recall vividly telling my parents we were expecting our first child and learning of my grandfather's death within minutes of one another. Similarly, I was never so fearful as the times my wife was in the midst of intense labor, praying for her safety and that of the baby's. And moments later, after one final push, being handed the most beautiful, healthy, and precious bundle of life.

❧

Do I understand how truly fleeting the joys of life can be or how quickly my sorrow can turn to celebration?

*I am forgotten by them as though I were dead; I have be-
come like broken pottery.*

Psalm 31:12

One of my responsibilities as an orthopedic surgeon
is to cover several nursing homes for those patients
with musculoskeletal problems. These patients are elderly and frail. Their bones are soft. Many have lost
their memories. They are often disoriented and confused.

But their failing health and general deterioration
were not the maladies I found so sad. What was most
sad was that these were forgotten lives. These octoge-
narians were removed from their families, their friends,
their own lives.

One of the saddest things I saw at one of the homes
was a bulletin board on a wall across from the nursing
desk. On it were pictures of the elderly patients from
their youth. There were prom pictures, wedding photos, graduation gowns. There were pictures of young
mothers surrounded by even younger children and
handsome men in military uniforms.

Sitting beneath those photos were the very same
faces, now old, wrinkled, wheelchaired, forgotten.
Those once vibrant lives were now withered bodies,
empty shells, broken pottery.

🕂

*Do I have the strength and the compassion to repair this
broken pottery and fill it with the love it once held?*

When I kept silent, my bones wasted away through my groaning all day long.

Psalm 32:3

I grew up in a home where the silent treatment was an accepted form of retaliatory behavior. If someone angered you, you just stopped speaking to them. When I began dating my wife, it was brought to my attention, painstakingly I might add, that this was not acceptable behavior. Not speaking to someone with whom you were angry made no sense to her at all.

It has taken me years to undo old habits. I still slip back into the silent treatment routine on occasion. But when you think about it, what sense does that make?

We all know that the key to a good relationship is communication. We hear this repeatedly from preachers, therapists, guidance counselors, even magazine articles. So why then are we so bad at it? How many times have we wished that we had told someone what was really bothering us? How many times have we kept things inside until they ate away at us? When I'm not speaking to my wife, I know it hurts both of us. It eats away at the core of our relationship and leaves us groaning for reconciliation.

⌗

How often have I held my tongue instead of expressing my true feelings?

No king is saved by the size of his army; no warrior escapes by his great strength.

Psalm 33:16

There are numerous accounts in the Bible of underdogs claiming spectacular victories. Armies vastly outnumbered by their enemies emerging victorious, Moses outwitting the pursuing Egyptian chariots, the Israelites defeating countless pagan nations, David felling the behemoth Philistine. These powerful, seemingly invincible entities were defeated by the small, the weak, the unsophisticated. Obviously these formidable foes harbored a false sense of power.

Likewise, we are all familiar with today's kings surrounding themselves with their own protective armies. Legions that they hope will save them from losing their power. Dictators have their secret police forces, politicians their loyal supporters, CEOs their VPs, junior executives and secretaries.

But to what end? To safeguard their positions? If they truly held the power, there would be nothing to safeguard. An honorable leader receives his power, not from force, but from those he leads. Anything less is a sham that needs protecting. Would any dictator remain in power if his subjects were not threatened into submission?

Do we do the same in our own lives? Are we husbands by brawn, parents by threat, bosses by fear? Is our leadership bestowed upon us or forced upon others? For if it is the latter, it will be very short-lived.

⌖

Does my strength come from within or is it derived by oppressing others?

Those who look to him are radiant; their faces are never covered with shame.

Psalm 34:5

My cousin, Bill, is a nurse at the Veterans Hospital in Brooklyn. He is also a practicing Christian. Several years ago a member of the hospital nursing staff was hospitalized and dying. She asked Bill if he would pray with her. At first, he felt awkward but he couldn't refuse her humble request.

While they were praying, Bill said the woman's face became radiant. He couldn't even look at her. She glowed. Her face was completely at peace. Her smile was relaxed. He described an appearance of utter contentment and serenity.

When they had finished praying, her aura returned to normal. She thanked Bill for praying with her. She died shortly thereafter.

Bill relayed all of this to me. He told me how blessed he felt that day. He said he was, without question, in the presence of the Lord, as was, no doubt, his dying friend.

✠

Am I open to the inner calm and the outward radiance that the Lord will bring me?

Take up shield and buckler; arise and come to my aid.
Brandish spear and javelin against those who pursue me.
Psalm 35:2–3

What is so fascinating about the Psalms is their ability to reflect multiple aspects of our own personalities. We have all been wronged at some point in our lives. We have all experienced the slanderous remark, the cheating salesperson, the unfair business deal. Undoubtedly, we have all prayed for vindication. We have begged for the demise of the wrongdoer. After all, as the saying goes, revenge is sweet.

But is it? Have you ever felt good after seeking revenge? Maybe for a split second. But that sweetness quickly turns to regret, to anger at oneself, to inner directed bitterness. We've stooped to the very same level as the person who wronged us and that is what so angers us. We thought we were better. We thought we were above all of that. But low and behold, I guess we're not.

That's why we need to pray. That's why we need the Spirit to guide us. We need the Spirit's power to soften our hearts, to hold the javelin before it's thrown. For once it leaves our hand, it destroys us, too.

※

Do I recognize, in myself, the desire for revenge?

For in his own eyes he flatters himself too much to detect or hate his sin.

Psalm 36:2

I think one of the easiest things to do is to turn a blind eye to our own shortcomings. It is so easy to find fault in others but we have such a difficult time seeing it in ourselves.

Even our language is replete with axioms warning us against this pitfall. People in glass houses shouldn't throw stones. Don't spit in the wind. Don't point a finger, three point back to you.

I think Jesus put it most succinctly, yet most powerfully in his two examples. He pointed out how obsessed we can become in finding the speck in our neighbor's eye while failing to see the plank in our own eye. And again, when the Pharisees tried to corner Jesus regarding the appropriate punishment for the young woman caught in adultery, he simply replied, "Let he who is without sin cast the first stone."

Could it be put any more clearly? None of us are blameless. So before we criticize, let's turn our eyes inward and examine our own behavior. Maybe then we can detect and hate our own shortcomings.

❄

Do I con myself into believing my actions are so pure that I fail to see my sins?

Better the little that the righteous have than the wealth of the wicked.... I have seen a wicked and ruthless man flourishing like a green tree.

Psalm 37:16, 35

I know someone who defines the word wheeler-dealer. Everything in this man's life is a scheme. There is profit to be made everywhere; opportunity abounds. The world is a game, a crapshoot, a roulette wheel.

Unfortunately though, it went beyond that. His connivings and dealings led to broken families. They ended in ruined lives. There were indictments, trials, more deals cut, more scams, more lives ruined. It went on and on.

I have to say, though, at the times he was riding high, I was envious. All of that wealth was so enticing. Couldn't I get just a little piece of it? Not the big score, just a little piece. Maybe invest in one deal, one scheme.

But we all know it doesn't work that way. It wouldn't have stopped at one investment. I would have gotten in deeper and deeper. The stakes would have been higher, the profits greater. And to what end? Another ruined family, destroyed lives, a wrecked marriage? No, thanks. I'll go the path of the righteous and earn my living another way.

❄

Am I so enticed by the prospect of wealth that I turn a blind eye to what is right?

My friends and companions avoid me because of my wounds; my neighbors stay far away.

Psalm 38:11

We have reached a point in our history where AIDS has become a reality for all of us. It is no longer a disease somewhere out there. It is no longer hidden in closets, spoken about in hushed tones, confined to that group. No, AIDS has arrived with a vengeance. It strikes our wives, our children, our friends. It is no longer the exclusive affliction of drug addicts and homosexuals. Hemophiliacs, postsurgical patients, health care workers, newborns, we are all at risk.

But regardless of the mode of acquisition, the fact remains that patients with AIDS die an agonizingly slow and painful death. They often lose friends, families, and finances. Their bodies wither. Their strength dissipates.

We cannot cure them. We cannot reverse this deadly disease. But we can comfort them. We can bring them companionship. We can converse with them, hold their hands, minister to them. Just being there for them can go a long way. Avoiding them will not cure their disease; it will certainly hasten their demise.

✠

Do I bring comfort to the sick, food to the hungry, companionship to the lonely?

You have made my days a mere handbreadth; the span of my years is as nothing before you. Each man's life is but a breath.

Psalm 39:5

As part of my orthopedic residency training, I rotated through Elmhurst Hospital in Queens, New York. Elmhurst is a city hospital. It is surrounded by four major highways. It is in the middle of one of the largest cocaine capitals in this country. It covers the Riker's Island jail. It is a Level One trauma center.

Needless to say, I saw my share of death and destruction, from train wrecks to machine gun retaliations. At a relatively young age, I was exposed to more death, especially in young people, than I would ever care to remember. I dealt with it. I never got used to it.

On one occasion, a young boy of nineteen came to the hospital for a dental extraction. During the procedure, he developed a severe allergic reaction to the anesthetic and died. One of the hospital social workers asked to use my small office to speak to the boy's family. I spoke with the social worker for several minutes before the family arrived. I shared with her my feelings about the constant and relentless body count we witnessed almost daily.

She shared with me one of the best pieces of advice I have ever heard. No philosopher, poet, mystic has come close with advice on the subject. She said something that changed my entire outlook on life and the way I now live mine. She simply said, "Jim, this ain't the dress rehearsal."

She was right. We get one shot at this. So live it to the fullest, enjoy every minute, because it is, indeed, only a breath of time.

✲

Do I realize how truly fleeting life is or do I plod along waiting for tomorrow to make it better?

Many, O Lord my God, are the wonders you have done. The things you planned for us, no one can recount to you; were I to speak and tell of them, they would be too many to declare.

Psalm 40:5

Have you ever witnessed the birth of a child? I don't mean on television or in the movies. I mean the real thing. Live labor and delivery. Screaming and pushing. Panting, blowing, breathing. Blood and pain all mixed together. And then the most spectacular miracle one could ever imagine, the emergence of a life.

A child is born. A living person is brought out of one person and into the arms of another. The whole concept is almost incomprehensible, literally, life from life. Who could have devised such a plan? In my wildest dreams, I could not have come up with this scheme.

I participated in the birth of all three of my daughters. I remember with utmost clarity, the intense labor before my wife delivered. At the moment of their delivery, I prayed harder than I've ever prayed before. I asked the Lord to keep my wife and my baby safe during those next few moments. They were.

What I witnessed during those births, what we experienced each time together, what the Lord had planned for us, I could never adequately express to you. I only pray that you be so blessed as to witness it for yourself. It is without question a miracle beyond belief.

✣

Do I realize how truly wonderous God's plans and works are?

Blessed is he who has regard for the weak, the Lord delivers him in times of trouble.

Psalm 41:1

Last Halloween my two oldest daughters were planning to go trick-or-treating with the rest of the neighborhood kids. Free candy is a big deal to kids. Parental consent to free candy is even bigger. Halloween, therefore, is a major childhood coup. Parental and dental restrictions are temporarily revoked.

In our neighborhood, the kids usually trick-or-treat in one large group. They find it exciting to be with their friends, as they collect their booty. On this particular Halloween, though, one of their friends was sick. Not just sick but sick enough to keep him from trick-or-treating. That's pretty ill.

When the rest of the kids in the neighborhood had completed their evening pillage, they met in front of the sick child's house. They rang his doorbell. When he came to the door, they all, each and every one of them, gave him a portion of their candy.

I have never been as proud of my kids as I was that day. Tears came to my eyes when my wife told me what they had all done. The boy's parents wept at his friends' generosity. But the kids thought it was no big deal. They never gave it a second thought. After all, it was just candy.

❈

Am I secure enough to share myself and my possessions with those weaker and less fortunate than I?

Deep calls to deep in the roar of your waterfalls; all your waves and breakers have swept over me.

Psalm 42:7

Several summers ago we were vacationing in Stowe, Vermont, with my wife's sister and her family. After several days, the kids were anxious for some adventure. The game room, swimming pool, and fishing pond were just not exciting enough.

One of the local townspeople told me of a nice little place to hike just off the main road. He said we would enjoy it immensely but he would not elaborate.

As directed, we found the obscure opening in the woods. We hiked the footworn path, heading deeper into the forest. After about a half-mile, the troops were beginning to grumble. "How much longer?" "Where are we going?" "There's nothing to do here." "Why did we come here?" I pushed them onward, hoping our local Baedeker was not trying to rid Vermont of some more pesty tourists.

Several hundred yards further we began to hear a faint rumble. We pressed on. The rumble grew louder. Our steps quickened. The rumble became a roar. Suddenly before us was a rock-lined riverbed with a crashing waterfall. The summer runoff was feeding the fall.

We carefully inched our way down the shale embankment to the water's edge. Sneakers came off. Socks were ditched. Pants legs rolled. We waded into the icy waters. The kids played for hours. The adults too. The water was as fresh and as clear as water could possibly be.

We returned to the falls two more times that week. The rushing waters and flowing stream provided a physical and spiritual cleansing for all of us.

Lord, can I appreciate both the immense power and invigorating refreshment of your waters?

Send forth your light and your truth, let them guide me; let them bring me to your holy mountain, to the place where you dwell.

Psalm 43:3

One year my wife and I decided to attend the Easter Vigil Mass with our young children. Our daughters were ages five and two at the time.

The Easter Vigil is held the evening before Easter Sunday. Prior to the start of the service the entire church is cloaked in darkness. All of the church lights are out. It's dark. It's real dark. It's also very quiet. There is a definite sense of anticipation as we wait in darkness for the resurrected Christ, the light of the world.

The rear doors of the church open and the Easter candle is brought into the church. Set against the unlit church, this candle's solitary flame is dazzling. Each parishioner is holding an unlit candle. From that single Easter candle the flame is passed from candle to candle, neighbor to neighbor. Within minutes the entire church is awash in candlelight. It is a magnificent sight to behold, from one solitary flame an entire community is aglow.

It was at this time, in the midst of silent, radiant flame, that my two-year-old chose, in her loudest voice, to sing "Happy Birthday." What better time? Thousands of lit candles. What better song? Everyone could join in.

The congregation laughed and then applauded her

song. What better time? The light of lights, the truth of truths, had just risen to conquer death. What better time indeed?

✵

Is my heart open to your light and your truth to guide me to your mountain?

Rise up and help us; redeem us because of your unfailing love.

Psalm 44:26

There was a small Albanian woman who wore a sari and lived in Calcutta, India. She lived among and cared for the poorest of the poor. Her name was Mother Teresa. She was a Missionary of Charity nun. In fact, she founded the order. She owned nothing and was as poor as the people she cared for. She shunned publicity and fame, yet she won the Nobel Peace prize.

While there have beeen volumes written about this perplexing, living saint, her message was one of blatant simplicity, "Do ordinary things with extraordinary love." Mother Teresa's life, it seems, was driven by one single force: love. She served the poor out of love. She cared for the sick and dying out of love. She sheltered the homeless out of love.

It was her unfailing love of God and God's unfailing love of her that drove her vocation. As she explained in her book *A Simple Path*, the more she served, the more she helped, the more she gave of herself, the closer she lived in God's love.

�֎

Are we able to love God unconditionally, knowing He loves us unconditionally in return?

My heart is stirred by a noble theme.

Psalm 45:1

Grover tries to understand the difficulties of being the new kid in school and lends his support to a new classmate. Angelina realizes the only way to achieve her dream of becoming a prima ballerina is through hard work and practice. She succeeds. Her family sits riveted in the audience as she performs.

I am amazed at the plethora of children's books available today. Not just silly kid stories but some really excellent children's literature. These books are superbly written. They have imaginative story lines and captivating illustrations.

What strikes me most, though, about these books are the profoundly deep and noble themes of which these authors write: honesty, sharing, self-sacrifice, generosity, friendship, selflessness, imagination, acceptance, and even faith.

I often find myself teary-eyed by the close of these heart wrenching dramas. This is usually accompanied by proclamations of, "Daddy's crying again."

So don't be fooled if these literary heroes are stuffed rabbits, blue monsters, or talking rodents. Their messages are as profound as any ever written.

❄

*Am I able to see the nobility in simple acts
of sharing, honesty, friendship?*

Therefore we will not fear, though the earth give way and the mountains fall into the sea, though its waters roar and foam and the mountains quake with their surging.

Psalm 46:2–3

One of the things I've come to appreciate about the Psalms is their exquisitely vivid imagery. I don't think many of us have experienced first hand, the geological upheaval described by the psalmist. A literary translation is, therefore, hard for us to identify with.

But all of us have experienced days that we would no sooner love to forget. I mean days from hell: the car didn't start, the kids were sick, a job was lost, a significant relationship failed. We've all had those days when the earth gave way and the mountains crashed into the sea. Genuine, personal cataclysms.

But somehow, we get through. We ride out the storm. We know the Lord is our refuge and our only hope is to put our trust in him. We have to. It is certainly beyond our resources to right mountains and calm seas, but He seems to handle the geology just fine.

❖

Can I put my trust in the Lord even when my life seems to be falling apart around me?

Sing praises to God, sing praises; sing praises to our King, sing praises.

Psalm 47:6

I have to confess to you that I love music. Not all music, mind you, but good old time rock and roll. I grew up on rock and I love it. I've tried other kinds. I've really tried to appreciate all types of music: jazz, classical, opera. They're not bad. I can understand their appeal but they just don't do it for me.

I understand that this is a very individual thing. Many people despise rock. It can be loud and annoying. It is often technically simplistic. But it gets me moving. One good song on the car radio can transform me from a listless, weary-eyed commuter to an energized, wheel-tapping racer.

Several months ago, I was treated to a magnificent event. I was invited to a rock Mass at my brother's parish. The service was fantastic. Young people, grade schoolers, high schoolers, playing electric guitars, drums, keyboards, and horns, all for the glory of God. They played their hearts out. The congregation loved it. We sang. We tapped. We rocked. We were uplifted.

Even my own kids, who often find Mass about as exciting as watching grass grow, were wide-eyed and captivated. I thank these young people for singing God's praises, in 4/4 time with wah-wah pedals and reverb.

✻

Can you feel the music in your heart and allow it to carry you closer to God?

As we have heard, so we have seen.

Psalm 48:8

We are a visual lot. For most of us, sight is our most powerful sense. Even the multitude of axioms regarding vision attest to this: seeing is believing, out of sight, out of mind, a picture is worth a thousand words. We rely heavily on the information we receive through our eyes. Smell, touch, sound, and taste just don't provide the same magnitude of input as does our sight.

It is no wonder then that we long for visual verification of our experiences. It is not enough to hear the music played. We want to see the performers in action. It is not enough for the food to taste good; its presentation completes the dining experience. It is not enough to smell our lover's perfume; we want to catch a glimpse of her beauty, too.

Likewise, is it any wonder then that we long to see God's face? We have heard His words, touched, smelled, tasted His creations, but still we long to see the creator. Our eyes cry out to see what our ears have heard. Yet Jesus put it best in his words to Thomas the Apostle, "Blessed are those who have not seen and yet have believed."

Are all of my senses open to the glory of God's creations?

Do not be overawed when a man grows rich, when the
splendor of his house increases; for he will take nothing
with him when he dies, his splendor will not descend
with him.

Psalm 49:16–17

My grandfather was quite wealthy. He was a mason when he came here from Italy at the age of seventeen. He worked exceedingly hard for his money. He was also an alcoholic.

While he was working, he kept his drinking in check. But once he retired, the wine bottle became his career. After my grandmother died, it became his best friend. My thoughts are that his drinking stemmed directly from his loneliness and his boredom.

One summer, when I was a teenager, I spent two weeks at his house doing odd jobs. I painted railings and fences, repaired chairs, cleaned out the shed. My grandfather checked on me hourly. He talked to me while I worked. We ate dinner together every night. He didn't touch the bottle once during my whole time there.

As his drinking increased, he became more possessive, more angry. He refused to leave his house other than to buy the newspaper. He didn't attend his grandchildren's weddings, his friends' funerals. He sat on his porch or in his driveway, like a sentry guarding his castle. His house controlled him. His possessions ruled him. The building was the envy of the block.

My grandfather died relatively young from alcoholic

cirrhosis. The house is still standing. The furniture intact. The railings painted. None of it went with him. It all stayed behind.

⌗

Do I count myself blessed by the number
of my possessions?

I will deliver you and you will honor me.

Psalm 50:15

 S o that is it? The essence of the entire covenant
boiled down to one single sentence? God delivers us;
we worship Him. Sounds simple enough. Clear, easy-
to-follow directions. So how come we've been screwing it up since the beginning of time? How come we
just can't seem to keep up our end of the deal?

God places us in a garden paradise where our every
need is met. We break the one simple rule He asked us
to follow. God freed His believers from slavery, even
divided a sea in half for their escape route. They returned the favor by resorting to pagan rituals, worshiping gilded livestock. God sent His son, His only son, to
save us, to renew the contract, to die for us. His best
friend denied he even knew him. His followers fell
asleep. His neighbors nailed him to a tree and killed
him.

How come we just can't get it straight? Maybe we
need a class in contract law. Maybe we need to hire
more lawyers. Maybe we need a more detailed agreement. We don't seem to be doing very well with
this one.

✠

*Lord, can I accept the simplicity of your contract
or am I too busy looking for loopholes?*

Wash away all my iniquity and cleanse me from my sin.
Psalm 51:2

When I was an altar boy serving Mass in my parish, I remember hearing the priest say those very words just prior to his reading from the gospels. He would ask the Lord to cleanse him so that he could worthily proclaim His gospel—His good news. It's hard to proclaim good news mired in sin. It's hard to rejoice and celebrate the joys of the resurrection, of forgiveness, of everlasting, unconditional love if one is cloaked in iniquity.

Even then, thirty plus years ago, I found those words fascinating. Lord, cleanse me, wash me, because I can't do much good if I am preoccupied with my own shortcomings. It's like that early morning shower that you need to get the day going. If we don't ask the Lord to wash away our sins, we'll be carrying around yesterday's dirt. That's some heavy baggage.

The Lord gives us a chance to start fresh. We all know that when we slip and fall, we get dirty. The Lord is offering us a chance to get up, wash off, and try it again.

✠

Do I accept the Lord's gift of forgiveness and His offer of a fresh start?

Here now is the man who did not make God his strong-hold but trusted in his great wealth and grew strong by destroying others!

Psalm 52:7

I never cease to be amazed by the timelessness of the scriptures. It is generally believed that the Psalms, traditionally attributed to King David of David and Goliath fame, were written as far back as 1000 B.C. Yet this verse could easily have been the opening line of a dozen stories in this week's *Wall Street Journal.*

Tell me this verse does not apply to the ruthless leverage buyout financier or the aggressive corporate raider. How many of today's companies have been plundered in hostile takeover battles? How many family-owned businesses swallowed by conglomerates, their CEOs prospering by destroying the work of others?

We seem to live in a world where getting ahead means doing so by stepping on the backs of others. The job is made even easier and less personal with computers and web sites. These pirates are not crushing small businesses. They are merely acquiring additional assets on an electronic balance sheet.

Even hospitals, our modern icons of health and well being, of philanthropic medical research, are swallowing each other up to expand their own catchment areas and eliminate competition. To what end? To better serve the health care needs of their surrounding communities or to satisfy the greed of their boards of trustees?

※

Lord, can my prosperity only come at the expense of someone else or do I realize that true wealth comes from letting go of my possessions, sharing all my blessings?

They were overwhelmed with dread, where there was nothing to dread.

Psalm 53:5

My oldest daughter refused to put her face in the pool for the first six years of her life. Now I can't get her to swim above water. My neighbor refused to try authentic Mexican food, strictly a meat and potatoes kind of guy. We forced it upon him one night in a restaurant. He ate his portion, his wife's, and is now seen strong-arming other unsuspecting friends into various Mexican eateries. My roommate in medical school would rant and rave about our histrionic, hysterical, loud, stupid, and inconsiderate Hispanic Harlem neighbors. He married an anesthesiologist from the hospital. She is Puerto Rican.

We all fear what we don't know. Whether it is simply entering a dark room or dealing with other racial or ethnic groups, we dread the unknown. And it is all of us. There is prejudice, hatred, and fear on all sides of the color lines.

It is certainly easier to avoid or criticize or, even worse, destroy that which we don't understand. Maybe if we would just take the time to flip on the light switch or try the water or taste the food or even reach across the color barrier, we would see there really is nothing to fear.

❄

Do I have the courage to lay aside my prejudice, in all its forms, and be receptive to the unknown?

Let evil recoil on those who slander me; in your faithfulness destroy them.

Psalm 54:5

The scenerio usually goes smething like this, "Dad, Kristen called me a jerk." My sarcastic reply, "O.K., I'll beat her." My daughter's response, "Good!" Then she waits as if the bashing is really going to take place. She is truly disappointed when her sister's annihilation does not come to fruition.

My guess is that the psalmist was not all that different from my kids. My guess is neither are we. We all revel in retaliation. We all want to see justice done, the enemy punished. We even ask the Lord to carry out the deeds for our own just causes.

But honestly, can the Lord take our requests any more seriously than I take my daughter's? Can we be deluded into thinking, even for a second, that His way is our way? Retaliation is our style, our pettiness, our shortcoming. I don't think asking the Lord to participate in our quest for revenge is going to get us very far. Maybe we need to open our hearts and listen to His way.

✠

Do I truly expect the Lord to carry out the desires for revenge I hold in my heart?

His speech is smooth as butter, yet war is in his heart; his words are more soothing than oil, yet they are drawn swords.

Psalm 55:21

I recently watched a television movie about the capture of Nazi war criminal Karl Adolph Eichmann. In the movie, the Masad agent guarding Eichmann in a makeshift Argentinian house-prison asks him why he did what he did knowing it was so evil. How could he follow this maniac, Hitler?

Eichmann's answer to the agent, paraphased, was that the agent wasn't there to hear his speeches. He wasn't there to hear the way Hitler could evoke a sense of pride that could make the listener do anything. A speaker so moving, so inspiring, that six million people would be killed by his oration.

St. James, in his epistle, writes so eloquently of the trouble our mouths can get us into. He compares the tongue to the small spark that can set an entire forest ablaze. He goes as far as to call the tongue a world of evil among the parts of the body.

And we all know all too well of that evil. How many times have we used our own words to criticize, hurt, and destroy? Or worse, how many times to deceive, to lie, to trick? Our words can seem as smooth as silk but can hold within them a burning fire. Maybe it's time to extinguish those flames with words of kindness.

※

Do I say one thing and really mean another?
Am I using words to hide hatred I may be
harboring in my heart?

Record my lament; list my tears on your scroll, are they not in your record?

Psalm 56:8

One of the most challenging roles bestowed upon parents is that of the highest ranking mediator and arbitrator in the household. There is rarely a dispute, argument, or altercation that does not require some parental judification. What amazes me though are the petitions brought before the court.

My daughters list every grievance, every wrongdoing, perpetrated by their siblings. As judge, I am expected to remember all of the previous infractions listed, not only remember, but have them catalogued and inventoried. "Dad, don't you remember she did that last time?" "But Mom, I cleaned the table three times this week and she only did it twice." "Yeah, but one time was really mine and you traded it because I walked the dog."

Where do they learn this? Obviously, from us. The psalmist tells us we do the same thing with the Lord. Does the Lord keep a record of every time we've been wronged?

I hope not because I know I'll show up on both sides of that list. Do I really expect the Lord to keep a daily scorecard of my tears and laments? I don't think so. I'm just happy He keeps me in the game.

*Am I preoccupied lamenting the times
I've been wronged?*

Be exhaulted, O God, above the heavens; let your glory be over all the earth.

Psalm 57:5

Not long ago I was in a plane flying home from lecturing in California. I had left the west coast in the predawn darkness. We were flying east into the sunrise.

About an hour into the flight, I peered through the small, postage-stamp size window across the aisle from me. The sun was just beginning to pierce the horizon. A thick carpet of clouds formed a surreal platform that the plane was skimming over. The sunrise suddenly exploded into the plane's window.

At that moment, I had no doubt in my mind whatsoever that God existed. The tranquil cloud cover, the morning darkness shattered by this tangerine fireball, all seemed to attest to God's creation.

I was enveloped by the sunlight, by His sunlight. I rode the cloud cover. I witnessed the birth of morning in all its glory. And at that moment, I realized that this was all too exquisitely beautiful not to have an all-powerful creator behind it. The earth was bathed in all God's glory.

Do I appreciate the glory of God and all of its splendor in the creations around us?

Break the teeth in their mouths, O God; tear out, O Lord, the fangs of the lions. Let them vanish like water that flows away; when they draw the bow let their arrows be blunted. Like a slug melting away as it moves along, like a stillborn child, may they not see the sun.

Psalm 58:6–8

Whew! Not much religious sentiment here. Smashing teeth. Ripping out fangs. Praying, no begging for revenge and vindication. How can stuff this brutal, this unchristian, be in the Bible? How could it not? Isn't the Bible about us, for us? It is a book, no, a collection of books, exploring our relationship with God and with one another.

So who among us has not felt these very same sentiments? Who among us has not had these very same desires? "Boy, I'd like to punch his lights out." "Oh, I wish he'd drop dead." "I'd like to scratch her eyes out for what she did." Different words, same sentiment. We've all been there. We've all wished ill upon our fellow man or woman. We've all prayed for revenge.

So you see, this verse is not from the psalmist. It is from us. We are the author. We are the spokesperson. We want the teeth broken, the fangs ripped out.

But before we judge others, though, let us look into our own hearts and see what darkness lurks there. For it is only in recognizing that darkness that we can begin to let in the light.

※

Lord, help me to see the darkness in my own heart, the plank in my own eye, before I criticize the actions of others.

For the curses and lies they utter, consume them in wrath, consume them until they are no more.

Psalm 59:13

I try to be as honest with my patients as possible. I don't want to worry them, needlessly, about each and every X-ray I take or test that I perform but I am always honest and forthright about test results, disease states, and patients' prognoses.

Recently, I was in a situation where the family asked me not to tell an elderly patient about his bone cancer. He had a very serious situation. His life expectancy, without treatment, was short. Surgery, chemotherapy, and radiation would certainly have extended his longevity. This kind of treatment, however, could obviously not be administered without the patient's knowledge.

The family said make something up. They refused to tell him about his condition. They refused to allow me to tell him. Instead of treatment, they bathed him in lies and deceit. As his condition worsened, their anger grew. And as it became harder to maintain the lies, their anger grew even more. Their lies literally consumed them in wrath.

✠

Do I lie and bury my head in the sand only to become angry at my own stupidity?

Give us aid against the enemy, for the help of man is worthless. With God we will gain the victory, and he will trample down our enemies.

Psalm 60:11–12

My cousin lay in a coma. He was forty-seven years old, young, healthy, two kids, beautiful wife. He played softball that morning, pitched a winning game, walked off the field and slipped into a coma when an aneurysm ruptured in his brain.

There was massive brain damage. The blood from the aneurysm destroyed large areas of brain tissue. Swelling and increased cranial pressure damaged the rest. The surgeons did all that they could. Medical support systems were exhausted.

Any chance of survival would not come from the men or women of the medical community. It could only come from God. At this point, medical endeavors were hopeless. Only God could provide this victory.

What I found most amazing about the whole situation was that everyone knew that. Physicians, nurses, family, children, all knew, and stated without hesitation, that Doug's only hope lay with God. The enemy, the aneurysm, had attacked. Only God could defend him.

That's the way it often is. Our only hope, our only chance at victory, is with God. The enemy is too overwhelming and our resources too limited.

⁂

When the odds are overwhelming, do I have enough faith to put my trust in the Lord, whatever the outcome?

For you have heard my vows, O God; you have given me the heritage of those who fear your name.

Psalm 61:5

One of the most frightening aspects of parenthood to me is the charge of spiritual development. God has given my wife and me the job of conveying to our children a belief in Him. And not just a belief but a sense that we are utterly helpless without Him. I don't mind teaching them to eat with utensils or to wash their hands after using the bathroom but this God stuff is scary. If I mess up, the consequences may be eternal. Where does one even begin the lesson?

Yet, since I have become a parent, my image of God has never been clearer. My understanding of selfless love, of unconditionality, of perpetual forgiveness, has never been greater.

Our success in teaching this lesson will become their heritage. That first seed that we plant will become the foundation for the growth of their faith. It is unlikely, though, that this lesson can be adequately taught with words. And if it were, those words would be quickly forgotten. No, this lesson is a lesson of example. If the Lord can be seen in our actions, our relationships, our dealings, then we have succeeded with the lesson plan. We have endowed our children with the heritage of believers.

❧

Lord, am I up to the task of spreading your word to those in my charge?

Do not trust in extortion or take pride in stolen goods;
though your riches increase, do not set your heart on
them.

Psalm 62:10

The newspaper was in rare form today replete with an assortment of horrific stories. One in particular stood out. Two brothers, one a former New York City police officer, used fake police shields to impersonate police officers and rob a local restaurant. The manager brought the men into his office, trusting their identification, and they robbed him. Their take was sixteen-hundred dollars.

Both men, according to the paper, were employed. Both had families. One was a former law enforcement official. All of those accomplishments are now tarnished. Jobs lost, families destroyed, reputations marred. For what, sixteen-hundred dollars?

What could they have been thinking? They trusted in stolen goods. They increased their riches. They set their hearts, but at what price? They destroyed their lives and, I am sure, those of their loved ones around them. And had they not been caught, is this something they would have been proud of? To show off their newfound wealth?

Yet, are these two any different from the thousands we see stealing in business, cheating on taxes, extorting monies from clients? And when the deeds are done, riding around in new cars, flaunting new money, as if it were honestly earned. Undoubtedly they take pride in these profitable endeavors. Undoubtedly their hearts are set.

❖

Lord, do I set my heart increasing riches irrespective of the means to get them?

On my bed I remember you; I think of you through the watches of the night. Because you are my help, I sing in the shadow of your wings.

Psalm 63:6–7

Nighttime can be frightening. I have probably evoked the Lord's name more at night than at any other time of the day. It is a time when children take ill and fevers tend to soar. It is a time when loved ones can be late in returning home. Every passing car brings additional anguish. It is a time when empty houses turn frightening, every creaking noise a potential intruder.

But the nighttime can also be a time of quiet reflection. A time to lie in the darkened stillness and feel God's presence. Mother Teresa said she began each prayer period with silence. It was not so much what she spoke to God but what God spoke to her during that silence.

So although our initial reaction to the darkness may be one of fear, it is a time we can use to be with the Lord. Let us listen, then, and feel the Lord during these night watches. Who knows? We may even come to embrace the night with joy instead of trepidation. We may even sing under God's wing.

⚜

Lord, do I use the quietness of the night to seek your presence and listen for your word?

They plot injustice and say, "We have devised a perfect
plan!" Surely the mind and heart of man are cunning.
Psalm 64:6

I had to testify before the grand jury today. It seems this physician in Manhattan was bilking Medicaid. He was ordering thousand-dollar knee and back braces for patients who didn't need them, and then not delivering them anyway. He billed for the goods but the patients never received them. Thank goodness they didn't need them in the first place.

As I sat in front of the grand jury, I thought to myself, how did this physician drift so far? I am sure, working his way through college and medical school, he held lofty goals and ambitions. How did he drift from the noble aspirations of the physician-caretaker to scamming his patients and the Medicaid system? When did the transformation occur? What made the cunning heart and mind devise the perfect plan?

I don't have an answer, but I do know that we are all capable of that mutation. Under certain circumstances, any one of us could have written those prescriptions. And to deny that, is truly the work of the cunning mind.

�֍

Do I preoccupy myself with get-rich-quick schemes in
search of the perfect plan?

You answer us with awesome deeds of righteousness.
Psalm 65:5

I was never quite sure which aspect of childhood Jesus had in mind when he instructed us to become like little children. I have a suspicion it is their sense of righteousness He was asking us to emulate. I know it must be, because I am so often awestruck by that quality in the deeds of my own children.

A case in point: I was sitting on the sofa, watching television with one of my daughters when a commercial appeared for an animal shelter in need of funds. Animals hold a special place in her heart. She carefully copied the address. She then went up to her room where she had been saving money for a much wanted music C.D. She took five of her nine dollars and mailed it to the shelter. No check, no hesitation, no second thoughts. Her justification, "They help dogs, Dad."

My kids do this often. Their generosity is impressive. I look at their unquestioning sense of righteousness and have no doubt in my mind that the Lord is teaching me through them. We often look to the heavens and ask, "Where is God?" He is answering us, not with parting seas or burning shrubbery, but with small children performing awesome deeds of righteousness.

⁂

Lord, can I see your presence in the small acts of kindness that surround me everyday?

*I will come to your temple with burnt offerings and ful-
fill my vows to you; vows my lips promised and my
mouth spoke when I was in trouble.*

Psalm 66:13–14

When my children want something from me, they will promise me the world. "Just buy me this, Dad, and I'll walk the dog every day." "Just let me stay up late this one time and I'll go to sleep early for a month." "Can't my friends come over now? I'll clean up my room tonight."

I suspect we do the same with the Lord. In times of trouble, we must make the most outlandish promises. "Just let me get this job and I'll give loads of money to the poor." "Just let this meeting go well and I'll go to Mass every Sunday."

I recently saw a cartoon in a magazine. A young couple were in a small rowboat, caught in a storm. The man was standing gesturing toward the heavens. The young woman was saying, "Don't promise Him anything else. I think the storm is ending."

I don't know if God is in the bartering business. I do know He loves us unconditionally. I also know we can never fulfill those promises. My hope is God understands that and loves us anyway. I suspect He does. I know I still love my kids, even though their rooms are a mess and the dog is rarely walked on time.

*Do I realize that the Lord loves me and asks for
nothing in return except my love?*

May God be gracious to us and bless us make his face shine upon us, that your ways may be known on earth, your salvation among all nations.

Psalm 67:1–2

We tend, as a people, not to do well with the unknown, especially those of us who are control freaks. And yet, God's plan is a mystery. His ways are not our ways.

My cousin's daughter was just recently diagnosed with leukemia. She is thirteen years old. This is her second cancer. The leukemia, it seems, is the result of the chemotherapy from the treatment of her Hodgkins lymphoma. As I pray for her and her family, I can't help but ask, "Why? Why Stefanie? Why her? Why two cancers? Wasn't one suffering enough?"

But who am I to even ask? I don't know the Lord's plan. As He tells the faithful Job, and I paraphrase, "You were not even there when I created the heavens and the earth. How could you possibly begin to know my ways?" We can't.

As the psalmist points out, it is only through God's graciousness that we might be allowed to know His ways. That's hard for us. To give up control is not in our nature. Unless of course, we trust Him implicitly.

✠

Lord, do I have enough faith to say,
"Thy will be done?"

...and from your bounty, O God, you provided for the poor.

Psalm 68:11

There is an organization in New York City called City Harvest. Its concept is rather noble. Surplus food is picked up from restaurants each night and delivered to soup kitchens and shelters throughout the city. This food would normally be discarded. Instead, it is used to save lives. From the restaurants' abundance, the poor are fed.

Sometimes I think that is exactly God's plan. He has provided us with plenty, but we seem to be messing up on the distribution end. We are a nation of plenty where thousands go hungry. Buildings abound yet the homeless live in boxes. We have walked on the moon but we can't walk through some of our own cities.

The question is not one of amount. Is there enough to go around? But rather, are we willing to pass it around? There's plenty. It's there. But we have to be willing to share it.

Many people interpret the miracle of the loaves and fishes as the infinite microdissection of dinner rolls and seafood. Maybe the true revelation is Jesus and the apostles compelling the people to share what food they had with them. To me, that is the miracle. To teach people to open their pockets, to open their purses, to reach out to the person next to them, and offer from their bounty.

Do I hoard my possessions or do I open my bounty and share that which I have been so abundantly blessed?

Save me, O God, for the waters have come up to my neck.

Psalm 69:1

I usually wake at five A.M. I am on the road by six. Although I have been following this routine for years, five A.M., still feels early. What amazes me, though, is the number of people up and going at this hour. By six there is already traffic on the highways. Many commuters have been on the road for quite some time. What time do these people get up?

We seem to be starting earlier, working harder, getting home later. My work day grows longer and longer. The pace is often frenetic. The pressures intense. One of my residents at the hospital commented to me, "There're just not enough hours in the day to finish all of the things I need to." She is right.

Where does it all end? How long can we keep up this pace, this pressure? There are some days when the waters are not only up to my neck but over my head. Interestingly, the psalmist felt this very same pressure long before the days of twenty-four hour banking, sixty-minute photos, and seven-days-a-week shopping. Imagine if he were around today. He would have to contend with deadlines and editorial boards.

✠

Lord, am I drowning under the pressures of everyday life? Am I running in place only to get nowhere?

May all who seek you rejoice and be glad in you.

Psalm 70:4

There is nothing quite as exciting as a new discovery. It can be as simple as finding a new restaurant or tasting a new dish. The sense of excitement at this newfound discovery causes us not only to want to go back for more, but to share our find with those around us. We will tell our friends, or better yet, invite them along the next time we go. It is almost as if we can relive that first experience through them. We look for the excitement in their eyes as they take that first bite.

The same is true for a newfound love. After that first date, we can't wait to be with that person again. We call, we juggle schedules, we rush through our workday, just to spend more time with them. We seem to be unable to get enough of that person. We want to spend every waking hour next to him or her.

It is with that same vigor that we should be seeking the Lord, that same excitement, that same enthusiasm. Not just on Sundays, or during times of trouble, but in our everyday lives, our everyday grind. Because we know the Lord is there, willing to be found, at any given moment.

✠

Do we seek the Lord with the same enthusiasm with which we pursue our other interests?

I will praise you with the harp for your faithfulness, O my God; I will sing praise to you with the lyre, O Holy One of Israel. My lips will shout for joy when I sing praise to you.

Psalm 71:22–23

During the summer between my junior and senior year of high school, I spent seven weeks touring Europe with twelve of my classmates and two brothers from the Marianist community. We traveled for several weeks and studied French at the University of Fribourg in Switzerland for the remaining weeks.

Munich, Germany, was one of our first stops. Being the tourists that we were, the Hofbrau House was a must see highlight. The Hofbrau House is a very large, German beer hall, catering mostly to tourists. Large, very large, Bavarian women would carry six to ten beer steins at a time, slam them onto the table top, then reach into their apron pockets for large salted pretzels. It was German beer hall partying at its best.

The hall was packed with tourists from every country. Feeling nostalgic for the good old USA, we began singing "Take Me Out to the Ballgame." Across the hall, another group of Americans heard us and joined in, then another, then another. Soon other countries began singing their national folk songs and compatriots joined from table to table.

It was fascinating. We found our kin folk through song. Other groups found theirs. It was these corny, folklore songs that brought us together. Everyone singing, everyone smiling, arm to arm in harmony. All from a few silly songs.

I wonder if heaven will be much different. Harps and lyres, singing and praising and shouting for joy. Sounds like great fun.

❈

Lord, do I appreciate the power of music to lift the spirit, join us in harmony and sing your praises?

All kings will bow down to him and all nations will serve him. For he will deliver the needy who cry out, the afflicted who have no one to help. He will take pity on the weak and needy and save the needy from death. He will rescue them from oppression and violence, for precious is their blood in his sight.

Psalm 72:11–14

When Mother Teresa died, her funeral was attended by tens of thousands of mourners. They came to pay their last respects. They came to pay homage. They came from every walk of life, kings and queens, bishops, priests, politicians, workers, beggars. The rich came. The poor came. They came from every nation. They all bowed to her.

Why? She had never offered them money. She had none. She could not grant them prestige. She shunned it. She had not wined and dined them. She begged for her own food. So why did they come?

They came because she had served them. They came because she put others before herself and God before all others. They came because she lived what they could only dream. They came because she embodied the words of Christ, to lead them is to serve them. To lord over them is to wash their feet.

Mother Teresa took pity on the weak, delivered the needy, rescued the oppressed. And it was for that, that all kings bowed down to her and every nation served her.

※

Lord, do I realize that the path to your kingdom is not on the backs of my brothers nor at their heads, but at their feet in perpetual servitude?

But as for me, my feet had almost slipped; I had nearly lost my foothold. For I envied the arrogant when I saw the prosperity of the wicked.

Psalm 73:2–4

My cousin is a federal Drug Enforcement Agent. He worked in New York City early in his career. After ten years of service, he decided to move his family to South Carolina. He felt he had to get out of the city. He felt he needed to be in a place where the law was respected and stood for something.

He told me agents would work for months planning a drug bust. Hundreds of manpower hours. For what? After an arrest, the drug dealers would be released and out on the streets before he even finished his paperwork. Bail money was posted from their pocket change. High priced lawyers were at their disposal. Literally, cartons of cash were available for their use.

Yet, if you're the one on this side of the law, how do you not fall prey to all of that? How do you resist the money, the cars, the women, the glamour, the lifestyle? It can't be easy. It would be naive to say it has no effect. Any one of us surrounded by all of that temptation might lose his foothold and slip. The prosperity of the wicked is certainly an attraction, not just in the narcotic world but for all of us. Fast, easy, big money is always a temptation. Our feet could slip at any time.

⌖

Lord, help me to keep my foothold amid the prosperity of the wicked. It is so easy to slip.

We are given no miraculous signs; no prophets are left,
and none of us knows how long this will be.

Psalm 74:9

A small baby survives after falling dozens of feet into a backyard well. Buried survivors are pulled from the California earthquake rubble days later with only minor injuries. A truck bomb explodes in the basement garage of the Twin Towers; the buildings remain standing. The majority of passengers survive the crash of a tumbling jumbo jet in the Midwest.

Those are the big ones. What about the little miracles we witness every day? A baby is born, a young child learns to read, complicated surgery is successful, a single parent doesn't lose her job, a small charity receives an unexpected donation. The list is endless. We have all experienced those small miracles of everyday life.

I know at times it can be very difficult to see the miracles. They are easily lost in the frustration and turmoil of our daily grind. But they continue to happen and they happen all around us. They may not be as spectacular as the lame man walking or the blind beggar seeing, but then again, they often are.

※

Do I lose sight of the miracles happening all
around me? Help me to recapture some of that sense
of amazement at the wonders of life.

To the arrogant I say, "Boast no more."

Psalm 75:4

My wife and I were car shopping. We were looking at everything. Some cars seriously, others, just because we like to look at cars. It's always fun to browse.

One afternoon we met at a dealership. It was a high end, foreign car manufacturer. We arrived separately since I was coming from work. Kathie had been at the dealership for quite a while before I arrived. She was miffed. Not one dealer had approached her the entire time she was there. She was certain it was a sexist thing, knowing that as soon as I arrived, the salesmen would come running. They didn't.

We continued looking, sitting in cars, opening trunks. No dealer. Five, ten, fifteen minutes. That's a long time in a dealership. An older gentleman entered the showroom wearing a full length fur coat. The salesmen were tripping over themselves to get to him. I had to laugh to myself. I had never experienced that degree of arrogance and superficiality in all my life.

We obviously did not fit the image this dealership was looking for to sell its cars. Despite what our needs, desires, or financial status may have been, our appearance deemed us unworthy to drive that particular brand of car. I'll have to rent a fur the next time we need a car.

⌖

In my arrogance, do I think myself better than others because of their appearance or their position?

His tent is in Salem, his dwelling place in Zion. There he broke the flashing arrows, the shields, and the swords, the weapons of war.

Psalm 76:2–3

It is interesting how the psalmist from centuries ago held the same hopes and aspirations as today's political leaders. As always, the Middle East continues to be a hotbed of conflict. Nations are perpetually on the brink of military retaliation. Horrific and cowardly acts of terrorism are committed weekly. Citizens on all sides live in fear.

Hopelessly, the politicians continue to shuttle back and forth making, what appears to be, miniscule advances in the peace process. Agreements are perpetually reached, only to be broken again. What happened to Kissinger's shuttle diplomacy or the Camp David Accords?

Sadly, I had to laugh, when the radio recently reported that President Clinton was meeting with the Israeli prime minister to see if he would agree to meet with the Palestinian Arafat. Word was, it was unlikely. Unlikely? How can peace ever occur when these two leaders can't even agree to sit down and talk to one another? Can there be any hope of reconciliation when two national leaders act like spoiled children?

Maybe the answer lies not in talk, but in prayer. Maybe the swords and shields, tanks and mortar rockets, cruise missles and sidewinders, will only be broken by the Lord.

❈

Am I infantile in my approach to conflict resolution, or do I make some attempt at understanding the other person's point of view?

Your path led through the sea, your way through the mightly waters, though your footprints were not seen.

Psalm 77:19

One of the most touching and popular poems is *Footprints in the Sand*. It is available in print, on plaques, in needlepoint, even on decorative china plates. There must be millions of copies of the poem in circulation. Why?

I believe that not only are the words beautifully written, but that they ring so true for all of us. We have all experienced those times in our lives, when the waters seemed unpassable, the sea about to crash upon our heads. We know, without question, it was the Lord who carried us through. It was the Lord who cleared a path for us.

We may have felt alone during those crises. We may have felt helpless. We may have felt abandoned, but in our hearts, we knew we were not. We did not march through those rising waters. We were carried.

Yet when we looked back, we never saw His footprints. At least we thought we didn't. So we patted ourselves on the back, and assumed we did it on our own. Once again, how little we know of the Father's ways.

✠

Do I have enough faith to trust the Lord's arms or do I try to march alone?

He remembered that they were but flesh, a passing breeze that does not return.

Psalm 78:39

My father-in-law recently passed away. I miss him terribly. We all do. He was a very dynamic man, always moving, always doing, always willing to help out.

He was also a lot of fun to be with. He teased the grandchildren. He broke chops mercilessly. He had fun with life and he made us all smile.

Of course, now that he is gone, we appreciate all the more, those traits that made him who he was. We miss terribly, all of those things that we loved so much about him. Without question, we regret that we didn't appreciate him more when he was with us.

Life passes quickly. The psalmist uses the metaphor of the passing breeze. Christ instructed us to enjoy the bridegroom while he is still here, because he won't always be with us. We all know these things. We all know that life is short. Yet we take for granted those around us, parents, spouses, children, siblings. It is only when they are gone that we realize the impact they had upon us.

Lord, do I appreciate the precious but fleeting nature of our lives?

We are objects of reproach to our neighbors, of scorn and derision to those around us.

Psalm 79:4

Over the past several years, there have been numerous church burnings throughout the south. Church burnings. You know how offensive churches can be, specifically, how offensive the people praying in them can be. Those people, so close to God, usually cause all sorts of problems.

There are repeated accounts of synagogues being vandalized and defaced. Synagogues. Temples. I guess houses of worship are offending a lot of people of late. It seems that people trying to stay close to their God are under attack.

But hasn't it always been that way? Evil seems to be a perpetual obstacle to finding the Lord. The devil went so far as to tempt even Jesus as he prayed in the desert. Undoubtedly, Satan is at work again in his attack on holy places. In these communities, he is pitting neighbor against neighbor to promote hatred and spread violence. Obviously, his tools are ignorance and intolerance.

We need to pray for these people, the victims and the perpetrators. We need to hold together as a community of worshipers. We need to stay focused on our desire to serve the Lord. He never said it would be easy.

⌖

Am I willing to incur the wrath of those around me in the name of the Lord?

You have made us a source of contention to our neighbors, and our enemies mock us.

Psalm 80:6

I saw a bizarre story on the news. It was Super Bowl weekend so football stories abounded. If you watch any football, you may have noticed a developing trend. Players huddle together before the game in prayer. They are not praying in churches or even in the locker rooms, but right there on the sidelines. They are praying in full view of the fans.

The National Football League, the story went on to say, is threatening legal action to stop this heinous practice. The league's position is that praying in public might offend some people. The involved players threatened to counter sue. As of now, the league has backed down and the players are still allowed to pray.

During a recent game that I watched, opposing players huddled together on the field to pray for an injured teammate. Paramedics worked for twenty minutes to stabilize his spine while the players prayed nearby. Today that player is fine.

We live in an age where tarnished players are a weekly news item: drug use, assaults, rapes, domestic violence, drunk driving. This is what our children are seeing in many of their sports heroes. But praying teammates are offensive and need to be stopped. We truly live in a world where right is wrong and wrong is right.

❄

Am I embarrassed to display openly my love for the Lord? Am I afraid of being mocked and reproached?

In your distress you called and I rescued you, I answered you out of a thundercloud; I tested you at the waters of Meribah.

Psalm 81:7

In the Hebrew Scriptures, when Moses was leading the Jews through the desert, there appeared to have been frequent complaints from the masses. Understandably, the journey was difficult; hardships were plentiful. When the people clamored in thirst, for water, it was at Meribah that Moses struck the rock and the Lord answered with refreshment.

Years ago, a large retreat house was donated to my high school. It was an excellent location for spiritual retreats, group discussions, or just quiet contemplation. It was a place to go to seek out answers to problems. And as we all know, adolescent problems are abundant. It was a place where God tested me and I sought Him.

In their wisdom, the religious community, who taught at my school, named the house Meribah. I knocked there often. The water always poured forth.

✠

Do I have a special place where I can go to seek the Lord, where He tests me and I find Him?

They know nothing, they understand nothing. They walk around in darkness; all the foundations of the earth are shaken.

Psalm 82:5

The White House is currently embroiled in scandal. President Clinton is being accused of an extramarital affair with a White House intern. This is in addition to two previous accusations of sexual improprieties. The executive office is abuzz with damage control measures and calculated responses. All sorts of rationalizations and hair-splitting semantics are being bantered about.

I guess the one response no one has considered is to simply tell the truth. That we certainly won't hear. We may hear shades of truth, because, after all, truth is a relative thing. Isn't it?

This is the morality currently being espoused by the leader of the most powerful nation in the world. Lying under oath is no longer perjury. Sexual relations with another woman, no longer infidelity. Preying on subordinate young women, no longer sexual harassment.

What message does this send to our young people, our allies, our foes? That we are truly a God-fearing nation, representing truth, honesty, and integrity? Who can possibly take us seriously? Who can possibly follow our lead when we ourselves are walking about in darkness?

Lord, am I a beacon for the rest of the world to follow or am I strolling about clueless?

Cover their faces with shame so that men will seek your name, O Lord.

Psalm 83:16

Charles Colson was one of the most powerful men in the United States. He was Richard Nixon's confidant, or more accurately, his hatchet man. All of that came crashing down, however, with the unraveling of the Watergate scandel. Colson was part of that whole mess. He was one of the major powerbrokers sent to prison.

Here was a man at the pinnacle of his political career brought to shame and ruin by his own greed. Mr. Colson recounts the story beautifully in his autobiographical *Born Again.* At the low point in his life, his career shattered, and personal catastrophe imminent, a friend guided him to the Lord. Colson tells how he sat in his car, outside his friend's home, and sobbed uncontrollably, praying for the Lord to show him the way.

It was only in his shame that Charles Colson found the Lord. It was only after losing himself, losing everything he had, that he was able to find himself. Colson spoke of a spiritual emptiness and searching for its fulfillment. Quite possibly, without his shameful downfall, he would still be searching. Maybe without his face covered in shame, the Lord would have continued to be a stranger to him.

⁂

Am I willing to lose myself in order to find myself?
Do I need to hit bottom before I am willing
to look heavenward?

Better is one day in your courts than a thousand else-where; I would rather be a doorkeeper in the house of my God than dwell in the house of the wicked.

Psalm 84:10

One afternoon I was able to leave work early. My route home takes me past our church so I was able to stop in for a few precious minutes of solitude. It was early afternoon. The church was quiet. The lights were dim. Sunlight filtered through the stained glass. I sat near the rear of the church, two or three pews from the back.

From the balcony, I heard repetitive, staccato, organ notes. Apparently, the instrument was being tuned. In the front of the church, an older gray-haired woman was arranging flowers around the altar. She worked slowly, precisely, adjusting each stem, then stepping back to assess her work.

In the set of pews to my right, across the main aisle, an elderly gentleman paced up and down each row. It wasn't until he turned that I realized he was pushing a soft dust mop. He took great care to cover every square inch of floor space. He worked slowly, carefully, patiently. There was no haste to his work. He was exacting in this simple, beautiful task. Undoubtedly, he took great pride in his work, in God's work.

I envied the utter simplicity of it all. I stopped into church for some quiet reflection, instead I was blessed with the pleasure of meeting the doorkeeper of the house of God. How truly fortunate I was that day.

❖

Am I content to perform the humble tasks of the Lord?

Righteousness goes before him and prepares the way for his steps.

Psalm 85:13

I have tried to imagine how John the Baptist must have been received by the people to whom he preached. I have a hunch it was not a warm reception. People don't like to be confronted by righteousness. They don't like to hear about making straight a path, about preparing the way, about following a road to redemption.

People don't want to change. People don't like to change. They don't like to hear about their faults and their shortcomings. I am sure they turned a deaf ear on most of the things John the Baptist wanted them to give up, change, rectify, and amend.

He forced them, and us, to face all of those things that must be made right for the Lord's step. Because like John the Baptist, we are not even worthy to tighten His sandal strap. Yet we must prepare ourselves to allow the Lord into our lives. We must be the righteous ones, preparing the way for Him to step into our lives.

✠

Can I clear a path in my life for the Lord to enter?

Teach me your way, O Lord, and I will walk in your truth; give me an undivided heart, that I may fear your name.

Psalm 86:11

One interesting aspect of the psalms is their ability to set lofty goals for us. They give us something to aspire towards, something to shoot for. We may reach our mark; we may not. Such is the challenge of this simple verse.

The Lord has made it abundantly clear what His way is. He placed us in paradise, asked us not to eat from one tree. We ate. He led us through the desert, asked us not to worship false gods. We fashioned a golden calf. He told us to love our neighbors as ourselves. We continue to sow hatred and distrust wherever we go. He told us to give up all we have and come follow Him. We guard our possessions tighter than ever. He told us the way to eternal salvation is through Him, with Him, in Him. We nailed Him to a tree and killed Him.

The Lord has taught us His way, and we have yet to walk in His truth. From the looks of things, we're not even crawling yet.

✣

Do I recognize all that the Lord has taught me and am I willing to walk in that truth?

He has set his foundation on the holy mountain.

Psalm 87:1

Mountain is one of those words that not only describes a geological entity but also evokes a personal sentiment in each of us. Mountains can be majestic; they can be frightening. They can be warm, lush, and green. They can be ice covered and forbidding.

Historically, they have always played an important role, providing some of the greatest challenges ever posed to explorers, pioneers, and advancing armies. They have literally changed the course of history.

Similarly, they have provided the setting for some of the most monumental events in biblical history. Moses received the ten commandments on a mountaintop. Noah's craft came to rest safely on a mountain. Abraham offered to God his most precious sacrifice, his son Isaac, on a mountaintop.

Likewise, Jesus was tempted, transfigured, and eventually crucified on a mountaintop.

Undoubtedly, some of the most defining moments in our religious history have occurred upon the majestic display of the mountaintop. The foundation of our faith truly began on His holy mountains.

※

Have there been mountains in my own life that have set the foundation of my growth?

You have put me in the lowest pit, in the darkest depths. Your wrath lies heavily upon me; you have overwhelmed me with all your waves.

Psalm 88:6–7

I met a patient today whose life was an utter tragedy. Actually, I first met her several years ago when I initially operated on her. She is young, in her early forties. She has already had several major operations, following a motor vehicle accident, including two hip replacements. She has very little money. She is a recovering alcoholic. There may also have been some drug use in the past.

She now lives with her mother-in-law, who has been diagnosed with breast cancer. The cancer is advanced, already spread to her bones. My patient moved in to help care for the woman. She feels an obligation to her mother-in-law because the woman's son, my patient's husband, is unable to care for his mother. He is in jail for drug possession and murder. There is also a nine-year-old daughter, who has only met her father through the glass panel of a prison visitation room.

My patient came to see me today for knee pain. She brought a cake for my office staff. Here is a woman unquestionably appointed to life's lowest pit. She has been dealt every conceivable blow, overwhelmed by every tragic wave. And yet, she takes the time to bring treats to an unknown group of office workers. I met a holy woman today. She came bearing gifts. She happens to be a patient of mine.

※

Do I have the strength to rise above my own misfortunes and put the feelings of others before mine?

I will punish their sin with the rod, their iniquity with flogging; but I will not take my love from him, nor will I ever betray my faithfulness.

Psalm 89:32–33

I was angry at my children yesterday. Actually, I was beyond angry. I was fuming. Not that they had done anything earth shattering, there were just a lot of little things building up, not doing chores, poor schoolwork, skipping piano practice.

I was simply tired of saying the same things over and over again. They were all well aware of their obligations and responsibilities. But kids will be kids, and parents will be parents. So I yelled and threatened and punished. Needless to say there was none of the flogging of which the psalmist writes.

Yet, although my disappointment was unmistakable, so was my unrelenting love. No matter how angry I may have been, I would never have dreamed of withholding my love. My heart is with them always. My support, my faithfulness is forever. My anger was but a fleeting instant.

❊

Am I able to separate discipline from chastisement, parenting from tyranny?

Make us glad for as many days as you have afflicted us,
for as many years as we have seen trouble.

Psalm 90:15

Fairnesss is a concept that takes on a whole new dimension when dealing with children. Whether it is chore time, permissible television viewing time, holiday gifts received or taking turns in the front seat of the car, those numbers had better be equal. In the juvenile scoring system, fairness is measured with a micrometer.

As adults, though, we are not all that different. We demand equitable treatment, equal rights and tit-for-tat retribution. We demand fairness on the job, in the marketplace, and in our relationships. We all want the playing field to be level, with each of us treated equally.

But God's way is not man's way. Our joys may be abundant and our sorrows rare. Or conversely, we may suffer catastrophic losses, with few joyful moments in our lives. We don't know the Lord's plan. We don't know what He has in store for us. We cannot demand equality. It's not ours to ask, just as we cannot demand equal gains or losses on our monetary investments. All we can do, though, is place our trust in the Lord. If we can truly do that, then tallying joyful days and sorrowful days becomes a moot point.

⚜

Am I so preoccupied with the scoresheet that
I miss the game?

*For he will command his angels concerning you to guard
you in all your ways; they will lift you up in their hands,
so that you will not strike your foot against a stone.*

Psalm 91:11–12

One of the pitfalls that one can fall into in following
the scriptures and in trying to lead the righteous life is
that we may begin to believe that we are better than
others. We are the good ones. They are the corrupt
ones. We follow the Lord's word. They stray from the
path. We are part of the Lord's fold. They are the lost
sheep.

It is easy to fall into that trap. It is easy to begin to
think that way. Once that happens, though, we grow in
our own importance. As soon as we believe that we are
better than those around us, then our arrogance becomes self-consuming.

Interestingly, it was with these very same words that
the devil tempted Jesus as He fasted in the desert. He
taunted our Lord with promises of an angelic rescue if
Jesus would throw himself from the temple peak. "If
you are who you say you are, then the angels will save
you." That's a dangerous trap to fall into, believing in
our own self-importance.

Jesus dismissed the devil. Would we be as strong, or
would we fall prey to our own arrogance? The devil
can easily con us into believing in our own self-right-

eousness. We need to pray for the strength to reject his temptation.

✦

Do I consider myself better than those around me, or do I understand that the Lord came to save us all, rich and poor, sinner and saint?

For you make me glad at your deeds, O Lord; I sing for joy at the works of your hands.

Psalm 92:4

There is a concept in Eastern philosophy that suggests that once we learn the name of something, we cease to ever see that thing again. For example, once we learn the word for squirrel, then every squirrel we see is the same. We no longer see the individual small, furry animal with the long bushy tail. We see the category. Every squirrel becomes the same. We fail to see subtle differences, nuances, characteristic traits.

We obviously need words. They simplify our lives. They allow us to categorize and communicate our ideas. They give us a handle on which to organize our thoughts. We could not possibly have a new name or launch into a lengthy description of each and every squirrel we see.

Yet once we learn the name of that category, we lose our sense of awe, of curiosity, of detailed perception of the individual. It is sad, because the works of the Lord's hands are spectacular. Each mountain, each river, canyon, monkey, or sparrow is a work of art. If we see "mountain," then we never see *the* mountain. I am always impressed with those biologists who can differentiate one lion from another by a small mark here or a scar there.

We need to take the time, though, to appreciate the variety and uniqueness of each creature. Words are helpful but they can dull our senses. We can't walk through life asleep to the wonders of the Lord's creation. Each sunset should be the first one we've ever seen.

❈

Do I realize the unique beauty of each of the Lord's creations including myself?

The world is firmly established; it cannot be moved.

Psalm 93:1

Most of our problems stem not from the world around us, but from our trying to change that world. The world is just fine, thank you. We are the ones trying to move the rock uphill. We are the ones trying to make reality conform to our notion of how things should be. We are trying to make what is and turn it into what we think it should be.

The opening line of the Serenity Prayer begins with, "Lord, teach me to accept the things I cannot change." It is interesting that we should have to pray for the strength to refrain from frustrating ourselves. Lord, keep me from banging my head against the wall. Lord, help me to accept things as they are, not as I want them to be.

The only changes we can effect are those within ourselves. We cannot change others. We cannot get them to stop smoking, or to lose weight, or to be more sociable. And we shouldn't. Those changes have to come from within. We should be striving to improve our own behavior, to strengthen our own inner selves, to come to our own peace.

How many people marry with the notion, "Oh, she'll change." Or worse yet, "I'll change him." It doesn't work that way. People do not change from the outside. We cannot make someone fit our notion of what a spouse or friend or parent should be. That world is fixed. We can choose to either accept it or not, but we cannot move it.

❈

Lord, can I allow the river of life to run its course or am I constantly trying to change its direction?

Unless the Lord had given me help, I would soon have dwelt in the silence of death.

Psalm 94:17

I saw a beautiful story on the news several nights ago. A wheelchair-bound woman was wheeling down a sidewalk in Harlem when something fell from a window above her, onto her lap. She thought someone had thrown something at her. In fact, though, an eighteen-month-old toddler had fallen out of an opened second story window. Undoubtedly, the child would have been killed or at least critically injured had it not been for the woman. Instead, he was saved with only a few minor scrapes. This invalid passerby had saved his life.

According to the news interview, she herself had been rendered paraplegic from years of drug abuse. The drugs destroyed her spinal cord and she eventually lost the use of both her legs. Her addiction apparently was longstanding and severe. Her family had given up on her. They severed all contact with her. Her doctors abandoned her and wrote her off for dead.

She said, it was at that point that the Lord came into her life. He carried her through. He gave her the strength to stop the drugs. He saved her life. And if you believe in the grand scheme of the Lord's plan, He put her in a place to save someone else's life. For without the Lord's intervention, two people would have been dead.

※

Do I have the courage to turn my life over to the Lord, to give to Him what I cannot handle myself?

Today if you hear his voice do not harden your hearts.
Psalm 95:7

I am convinced that children are afflicted with a condition known as selective deafness. It may be an inherited disorder, but somehow I think it is an aquired trait. I don't think it is the result of loud music or other environmental noises. I also think it spans several generations. My wife says I have it, too.

I am sure you are aware of the condition. The child is called, called again, called more forcefully. No response. Now you're yelling at the top of your lungs. "What? Were you calling me?" Yet this is the same child who will materialize from three rooms away as you're whispering something secretive to your spouse. "Who said she couldn't stand Mrs. Smith's daughter?"

I do not think that this form of deafness is a neurological condition. I think it is, most likely, a form of distraction. They are too busy, too engrossed, with their own agenda, to be bothered with your summons. Television, friends, music, magazines are all infinitely more important than anything for which you might be calling.

I do not think it is all that different with the Lord. Our lives are so busy, so important, so demanding. Who could possibly hear the Lord's call? We are so distracted and preoccupied that His call often goes unheeded. I think we need to listen more carefully or we are going to wind up missing some dinners.

✠

*Am I too distracted to hear the Lord's call
in my daily activities?*

Sing to the Lord, praise his name; proclaim his salvation day after day. Declare his glory among the nations, his marvelous deeds among all people.

Psalm 96:2–3

My oldest daughter was recently watching a music awards show on television. She was anxiously awaiting the performance of one of her favorite performing artists. I stopped in front of the T.V. to catch a glimpse of the winning group in one category or another.

The awards hall was packed with celebrities from all nations. The performers, the nominees, and the audience members were dressed as only musical artists can dress. One outfit was more outlandish than the next. Hairstyles were often a cross between electrical shock and army bootcamp. It would have been so easy to dismiss the whole lot as a bunch of kooks, living on the fringe.

Yet, as the winning group took the stage, to accept their award, their acceptance speech began, "We like to thank, first of all the Lord, Jesus. We wouldn't be here without Him." I continued to watch. By the end of the program, a large percentage of those "kooks" had thanked the Lord. Kooks? Maybe. On the fringe? Probably. But how many of us would have the courage to stand in front of thousands and publicly praise the Lord for our blessings? How many of us would declare God's glory among all peoples? I was glad my daughter was watching.

⚜

Do I take the time to thank the Lord, to declare His glory, His marvelous deeds, day after day?

All who worship images are put to shame, those who boast in idols, worship him, all you gods.

Psalm 97:7

When I was younger and I thought of people worshiping idols, false gods, I envisioned a group of gypsy-clad pagans, chanting around some guilded icon, as a fire burned off to the side. As I've grown older, though, idolatry does not seem so foreign, nor so primitive.

Any one of us who puts money or possessions ahead of the Lord is guilty of image worship. Anyone who steps on the heads of those around him, in order to elevate his own stature, is an idolater. People are literally killing each other over Rolex watches, dented automobiles, and ATM cards.

We have set up money, stature, fame, possessions, and power as our gods and we will not hesitate to sacrifice anything to service those gods, including family, friends, or principles. Ironically, in and of themselves, those objects mean nothing. There is nothing wrong with owning an expensive watch or driving a fancy car, but when we become obsessed with possessing them, then they have become our own golden calves.

⌗

Can I enjoy the nice things that I own without becoming obsessed with them?

The Lord hath made his salvation known and revealed his righteousness to the nations.

Psalm 98:2

I believe the Bible must be the most widely published book in the world. There are innumerable versions, editions, and formats. There are childrens' Bibles, teen Bibles, study Bibles. God has certainly spared no ink in letting know His ways, in letting us know the path to the Lord.

But who is reading? Who is listening? More importantly, who is living them? We have been given the instructions, the plans, the blueprints, but are we following them? In the Bible-rich south, there are still church burnings and lynchings. Nation after nation, with vastly Christian populations are acting in the most barbaric and paganistic manner.

Still, people are complaining, "I don't know God." "How do I know God exists?" Well just how many more of His best sellers do we need to publish before we recognize His presence? I think the Lord has done His part to make known His ways. We are the ones who have to open our eyes and more importantly, our hearts, to live His challenge.

✠

I know God's plan. I understand His salvation. What more am I waiting for before I live His words?

O Lord our God, you answered them; you were to Israel
a forgiving God, though you punished their misdeeds.

Psalm 99:8

As we move through life, our image of God changes, at least it did for me. When I was a young boy, I pictured a bearded, imposing figure, sitting upon a formidable throne, tallying my rights and wrongs. In high school and college, the Lord became my friend, someone to hang with, someone to bounce my ideas off of, someone to condone my adolescent behavior.

Now, as a parent, my perception of God has changed once again. The image of the father seems most appropriate. I can now begin to understand for the first time, the concepts of unconditional love, infinite forgiveness, perpetual acceptance. I can take to heart those sentiments the biblical authors portray so vividly: joy at the creation of new life, pride in their growth and development, anger and frustration when they reject your ways, and sorrow when even one small sheep is lost.

Throughout history, God punished the people of Israel, yet waited perpetually with open arms. Can we be any different as parents? Do we not guide with loving sternness? Punish with the hope of instructing? Accept with unconditional love? To do that, as parents, is to grow ever closer to an understanding of the Lord.

✠

Can I remain perpetually forgiving even after
I have been repeatedly wronged?

Know that the Lord is God. It is he who made us, and we are his; we are his people, the sheep of his pasture.

Psalm 100:3

I was crossing Sixty-third Street in Manhattan. Standing on the corner, next to me, was a disheveled looking, apparently homeless man. We both crossed the street when the light changed. We were walking almost next to one another.

As he was about halfway across the street, he must have stepped into the path of an on-coming young woman. She was forced to alter her path several inches to avoid a collision. As she passed the homeless man, she looked at him in utter disgust. Her glare held this man in complete contempt. The scowl was not lost upon the man. He turned to the woman but was now speaking to her passing back. "How much can you possibly hate me?" he questioned.

I felt his pain in my heart. How could this man, who this woman never met, provoke such hatred? It was clear that his very existence disgusted her. He had done nothing other than pass her on the street. Obviously, that was enough.

⁜

Do I sometimes forget that we are all sheep of the same pasture with but a single shepherd?

My eyes will be on the faithful in the land, in that they may dwell with me; he whose walk is blameless will minister to me.

Psalm 101:6

It is interesting how small, seemingly inconsequential acts stick in our minds.

When I was in high school I had a bulletin board hanging on the back of my bedroom door. My mother cut out a quotation from a newspaper article and pinned it to the board. It read, "A man grows with the company he keeps."

She was very concerned, as all parents are, with my growth and development. She also knew that a major part of that growth would be influenced by my friends. Especially during the teenage years, peer pressure can be enormous.

John was a close friend throughout grammar school. We both loved animals and had wanted to become veterinarians. We went to different high schools and grew apart. John associated with a group of peers much less interested in pursuing animal studies. His grades dropped and school became less important. Sadly, John was killed on a local avenue while drag racing with his newfound friends.

To a teenage boy, my mother's choice of quotations seemed corny; it was, after all, the sixties. "Make love not war," "Give peace a chance," and "Drugs, sex, rock-and-roll," were in vogue. But she knew that my choice in friends would have far greater consequences on my life than I could ever appreciate at that age.

❖

Do I have the courage to follow the faithful and the blameless?

Hear my prayer, O Lord: let my cry for help come to you.
Do not hide your face from me when I am in distress.
Turn your ear to me; when I call, answer me quickly.

Psalm 102:1–2

Several years ago I was scheduled to perform knee surgery. My patient was a rabbi. As he lay on the stretcher outside the operating room before surgery, we chatted. He was anxious about his surgery and rightfully so. I explained to him that although I perform several procedures a week, I too was nervous when I had to have my own surgery. It is a normal reaction to something unknown and something potentially dangerous.

The rabbi then turned to me and asked if I prayed before surgery. The question caught me by surprise, not because of its straightforwardness, but because I did indeed say a little prayer before each procedure. I told him that I did pray. I told him that I ask God for strength and guidance during the surgery. I ask God for His help. I ask Him to keep me out of trouble and to let things go smoothly. I then tell the Lord, "It's in your hands. You are the surgeon. I am the instruments."

"O.K.," said my rabbi-patient nodding. "Let's go in." And so we did.

⌖

Can I place my trust in the Lord and allow Him to
perform His works through me?

As a father has compassion on his children, so the Lord has compassion on those who fear him: for he knows how we are formed...

Psalm 103:13-14

It is fascinating how children's personalities are developed at such an early age. When my middle daughter was just two years old, she was standing on the steps of a pool, with my nephew. My brother-in-law and I were sitting at the other end of the pool talking. Suddenly, my daughter walked down the pool steps and into the water. Although she was at the shallow end, the water was still over the head of a toddler. My nephew reached in, grabbed her by the hair and pulled her to safety. We ran over to help.

I was frightened. It all happened so quickly. She was startled. Seeing that she was fine, I began the obligatory parental interrogation. "Alaina, what did you do?" as if what she had done was not abundantly clear. "Water, Daddy." "Yeah, water," I replied. "You went under the water. Are you O.K.?" "Scared, Daddy." My reply, "Yes, scared. Are you going to do that again?" Then came the answer that illuminated for me, the personality my daughter would have for the rest of her life, and more frighteningly, for mine. "Probably."

Probably. Probably. She was just under water, could have easily drowned and she said she was probably going to do it again. I knew in that defining moment, all that I would need to know about that child's personality. In that three syllable response, I knew exactly how she would develop. To this day, she has not let me down. Her love of life, her love of adventure, still outweighs her sense of personal danger. As her guardian, as her father, all I can do is love her for it, and hopefully watch over her.

Do we realize that the Lord knows us better than we will ever know ourselves?

How many are your works, O Lord! In wisdom you made them all; the earth is full of your creatures. There is the sea, vast and spacious, teeming with creatures beyond number —living things both large and small.

Psalm 104:24–25

At a party, I was approached by a young woman with some serious questions about science and religion. She knew that, as a physician, my education was largely scientifically based. She wanted to know my views on topics such as evolution. How did I justify my scientific background with my religious beliefs?

I explained to her that I had little difficulty with the issue. Yes, I did believe in evolution, as a theory. Scientific evidence of species evolving and changing seemed convincing. But, even scientifically, evolution could not be the sole explanation for the origin of life and the development of species. The more science I have studied, the more convinced I am of a divine creator. I could not fathom the biodiversity and complexity of life on this planet being explained by a single scientific theory. That diversity could only come from a divine creator.

And why could God not use evolution as a tool? Why could He not intervene at any step in the evolutionary process? If evolution is the only explanation, then where are all of these intermediary species? Have they all died off?

No, evolution is a theory. It is interesting. It is plausible, but it is filled with gaps and unexplained phenomena. It clarifies some interesting scientific questions, but it does not, in any way, replace my beliefs in a divine creator. Most importantly, it does not jeopardize my faith in the Lord.

⌗

Am I able to reconcile some of the fascinating, scientific discoveries of our time with my beliefs and faith in the Lord?

Give thanks to the Lord, call on his name; make known among nations what he has done. Sing to him, sing praise to him; tell of all his wonderful acts.

Psalm 105:1–2

The baby cuts her first tooth; grandma is called. Your daughter is accepted to a prestigious college; all of your friends know. You buy a brand new sports car; drive around the block so all the neighbors can see. We are proud of life's joyous moments, its crowning achievements. We like to share those moments with those around us, and we should.

But do we also share the Lord's wondrous deeds? Do we give equal time to His achievements? Do we tell every nation what the Lord has done? You know, the small things like creating the heavens and the earth, the millions of species of plants and animals, promising to us His kingdom in heaven.

It's fun to brag about the good things that happen to us, the promotions, the cars, the achievements. That's the easy stuff. It is much harder though to brag about the good news of the Lord, His wondrous deeds, His creations, His unconditional love for us.

But don't hold back. I've seen the Lord's work. It's pretty impressive. So brag away. Sing of His wonderful acts.

❧

Am I awe inspired by the works of the Lord, from the smallest grain of sand to the highest of mountain peaks?

*They did not destroy the peoples as the Lord had com-
manded them, but they mingled with the nations and
adopted their customs. They worshiped their idols,
which became a snare to them.*

Psalm 106:34–36

At a recent Bar Mitzvah ceremony, I had the pleasure
of listening to a dynamic guest speaker at the syna-
gogue. His name is Dennis Prager. Dennis is a radio
personality and author from California. He is quite
outspoken about the demise of spirituality in our society, specifically, the loss of Jewish tradition to secular
mores. As I listened closely to his message, though, I
realized that his words apply to all of us, Jewish or
not.

Mr. Prager spoke, quite forcefully I might add,
about political leaders abandoning their faith in the
name of secular rights. He gave the example of a Jewish congressman from the south who was the only dis-
senting vote in a referendum suggesting that businesses
post a copy of the Ten Commandments in the workplace. The mere suggestion of a religious code of ethics
in the workplace might offend someone.

Dennis also spoke about parents afraid to discipline
their children. We have become so fearful of offending
anyone that we refuse to call right, right and wrong,
wrong. The Lord's instructions are very black and
white, but society seems to have whitewashed our con-
sciences in every possible shade of gray.

This nation was founded by God-fearing men who

incorporated their beliefs and their theology into our government and our laws. It seems that society is doing all that it can to abolish that foundation.

※

Have I lost sight of my spirituality and become blinded by a society driven by secular beliefs?

Then they cried to the Lord in their trouble, and he saved them from their distress. He sent forth his word and healed them; he rescued them from the grave.

Psalm 107:19–20

I recently met Mary Magdalene. She was referred to my office needing possible knee surgery. She was a young hispanic girl who told me she twisted her knee while working as a dancer. I imagined Lincoln Center or Broadway. She was in fact, an exotic dancer, a club dancer, a stripper.

When she returned for her second office visit to discuss surgery, her boyfriend accompanied her. He was large, obnoxious, and controlling. He made every attempt to dominate the examination and consultation.

The dancer eventually came to surgery. After surgery, I had to deal with the boyfriend again. He continued to be large, obnoxious, and controlling.

On her first postoperative visit the boyfriend was not present. I took the opportunity to voice my opinion of him. Apparently, it went beyond obnoxious. He was forcing her into sexual relationships with several of his friends. He was using her as a toy. He wanted her to have his child so she would become even more dependent and indebted to him. I spoke to her at length. I was forthright and honest. She struck me as a bright girl with a good heart. She was a lost sheep.

On her final visit, she came to the office with a cross around her neck. She said she needed to get her life together. Last I heard from her referring physician, she left New York, left the boyfriend, and returned to school. I met Mary Magdalene recently, and just as she did 2000 years ago, she showed me that the path to the Lord is not always a straight one.

✠

Do I realize that it is only with the Lord's help that I will be rescued?

Give us aid against the enemy for the help of man is worthless. With God we will gain victory and he will trample down our enemies.

Psalm 108:12–13

It is not unusual to hear of patients dying of incurable cancers. All known medical treatments have been exhausted. Conventional and not-so conventional modalities have failed. Surgery, radiation, chemotherapy have been unsuccessful. In desperation, these patients simply turn their fate over to the Lord.

Many are cured. There is no explanation, at least no physiologic or medical explanation. The doctors are often baffled. The experts surprised. But when one sees an interview with the patient or reads an account of the patient's ordeal, the patient is not at all surprised. Their faith is unshakable. Their cure was simply and miraculously a gift from God, nothing more, nothing less.

Why one patient is cured while another dies is certainly beyond the scope of these reflections and even beyond the scope of human understanding. We don't know God's plan. But we do know that without His help, our victory against incurable cancer would fail. In all of these cases, medical intervention was worthless. Only the Lord could trample this particular enemy.

✠

Do I have the courage to place my fate in the hands of the Lord?

For wicked and deceitful men have opened their mouths against me; they have spoken aginst me with lying tongues. When he is tried, let him be found guilty, and may his prayers condemn him. May his days be few; may another take his place of leadership. May his children be fatherless and his wife a widow.

Psalm 109:2, 7–9

We purchased a pool for our backyard. Actually it was more of a sideyard than a backyard. The pool was nothing fancy or elaborate. Something for the kids to cool off in the summer.

The pool was ordered but never arrived. First one week late, then two. Summer marched on. Once delivered, it was never being installed. The days passed. The temperature increased. Precious summer days wasted while the pool sat in boxes.

I became furious at the pool people. My anger grew into hatred. I literally began to despise these people over a pool. I found myself wishing ill of this man. I wished nothing but vengeance and retribution on him, on his family, his store, his livelihood. I wanted nothing more than to see his business ruined.

But then I caught myself. I was seeking revenge over a pool. What was I thinking? What had gotten into me? In my hatred, I felt so unchristian, so undeserving of God's love. Was my way God's way? Is this what I had learned?

I wanted nothing more than revenge. God wants nothing more than for us to love one another. So what's it going to be? His way or our way? Not much of a quandary there. I thanked the pool man when it was finally installed, told him he did the best he could, even tipped the workers. I notice I swim a lot better without all of that weight.

�֍

Am I suffocating myself in seeking
retribution and revenge?

Your troops will be willing on your day of battle.

Psalm 110:3

My oldest daughter just completed her middle school education and now moves on to the high school. I loved her time at the middle school. The principal there was an extremely intelligent and caring individual. He knew that his job and that of his faculty was not just educating my daughter scholastically but educating her for life.

His major concern for these young adolescents was not their future SAT scores but rather preparing them for the life altering decisions they would soon be making. He knew that in the very near future these kids were going to be tested. They would be confronted, if they already were not, with decisions about drugs, alcohol, sex, and all sorts of other temptations.

Frighteningly, the choices they make could be a matter of life and death. More than likely, their parents will not be there when these situations arise. These kids, children really, will be at battle with forces literally trying to kill them.

Will they be ready? Will their troops be prepared? I pray they will. And I am glad that my daughter had an educator who did all that he could to train his troops for these battles.

⚔

Am I prepared to do battle for the Lord against those who seek His destruction and mine?

Great are the works of the Lord; they are pondered by all who delight in them.

Psalm 111:3

As a physician and surgeon, my work place is the human body. I study it. I observe it. I treat it. I dissect it. I operate on it. I care for it. I have been doing these things for quite some time now and not a day goes by that I am not totally amazed by its function and design.

We are a spectacular creation. Our bodies have a protective layer that guards against hot and cold, wet and dry. The layer even repairs itself when damaged. It has an immune system that rivals any military force in the world, capable of seeking and destroying even the most microscopic of enemies.

Its command center harbors more electrical circuitry than all of the P.C.s in the world combined. Its structural system is engineered for strength, motion, protection, mineral storage, and cell production. It has a hydraulic pump that runs day and night, for decades, usually without repair. And it can be fueled with almost anything from caviar to Twinkies.

We build machinery, electronics, appliances, and call them spectacular, incredible, magnificent. The Lord created us and said it was good.

❖

Lord, do I marvel at your creations and delight in their magnificence?

He will have no fear of bad news; his heart is steadfast,
trusting in the Lord. His heart is secure, he will have no
fear; in the end he will look in triumph on his foes.

Psalm 112:7–8

I heard a sad, actually heartwrenching story on the news. There was a house fire in a town in New Jersey. Several people were killed in the fire, an elderly man and two young boys.

It seems the man was the grandfather of the boys. Apparently, according to witnesses, he had escaped the fire to the safety of the sidewalk. When he realized, however, that his two grandsons were still trapped inside, he reentered the burning building to save them.

The firefighters found all three bodies only several feet from safety. The boys were clutched in the arms of their grandfather. He did his best to get them out but was overcome by smoke and flames.

I was obviously saddened by the story and by the deaths of three innocent people. Yet, this single act of selfless heroism totally restored my faith in humanity. The grandfather, obviously without thought of his own safety, put the lives of two small boys ahead of his own.

We don't see much of that nowdays. In these times of me-first attitudes, selflessness is a rarity. I could not help but recall the words Jesus spoke to the thief cruci-

fied on the cross beside him, "Today, you will be with
me in paradise." I am sure those boys and their grandfather are.

❈

Can I be fearless, putting my trust
in the Lord?

He raises the poor from the dust and lifts the needy from the ash heap; he seats them with princes, with the prince of their people.

Psalm 113:7–8

There was a very heartwarming story in *People* magazine. (Yes, I confess, I enjoy reading *People*). A woman, Mimi Silbert, from San Francisco, founded a program to train ex-convicts in a variety of occupations ranging from chefs to printers. All of the residents must earn a high school diploma. All of them are trained in manual, clerical, and public relations skills.

Society had essentially given up on these individuals. Many were homeless and in the dust. Most had driven their lives into the proverbial ash heap. All of them were in trouble. All of them had significant blemishes on their police records. Most employers would not take a chance on such a person.

But Mimi did. She saw through the misdemeanors and felonies. She looked beyond the immediate and saw what could be, who they really were. Most importantly, she acted upon that vision. Most of us would not have. Most of us would not see the person in the ash heap and envision him sitting with princes. Maybe it's time we start revising our seating arrangements.

❖

Can I look past an individual's faults and shortcomings and see the genuine person that the Lord created?

The sea looked and fled, the Jordan turned back; the mountains skipped like rams, the hills like lambs.

Psalm 114: 3–4

Volcanoes, tidal waves, earthquakes, tornados. In biblical times, these events would have been thought to be the work of God but we are a modern, sophisticated lot. We have scientific explanations and theories: geological shifts, changing weather patterns, meteorlogical events.

Those may be true. I do not have an answer. I know we spend billions on scientific equipment yet earthquakes hit without warning. I know we have satellites watching every cloud drifting our way and hundreds are killed by storms. I do not pretend to know what is God's hand and what is not.

I know that we can predict little of nature's upheavals. I know God's ways are not our ways. I know He created the heavens and the earth. Why should they not move at His command?

I truly feel that little in my life has occurred without the Lord's guidance. I cannot believe that His same hand is not at work in nature. We look to the mountains and the oceans and we marvel at the Lord's spectacular creations. Yet when these same oceans move, we cry El Nino.

Am I able to see the Lord's hand at work in nature today?

But their idols are silver and gold, made by the hands of men. They have mouths but they cannot speak, eyes but they cannot see; they have ears, but cannot hear; noses but they cannot smell; they have hands but cannot feel; feet but they cannot walk; nor can they utter a sound with their throats. Those who make them will be like them, and so will those who trust in them.

Psalm 115:4–8

The grandson heir to the Gucci clothing dynasty was killed by hired assasins. His ex-wife, Patrizia Reggiani, is accused of hiring the gunmen. It seems the marriage had gone sour.

More importantly, though, the grandson was apparently mismanaging the clothing empire. Profits were declining. Cutting edge designs were a thing of the past. Money was tight. In her divorce settlement, Reggiani had to make do with a mere $150,000 a month. Some months her husband sent as little as $90,000.

The limited stipend left Patrazia financially strapped. How could she maintain her lifestyle on such an austerity budget? After all, this was the same woman who told reporters, "I would rather cry in a Rolls Royce than be happy on a bicycle."

Is that not the saddest statement you have ever read? This woman would rather be rich than happy. She would choose to live in extravagant misery than simple contentment. She undoubtedly has become as lifeless as those gold and silver gods she so obviously worships.

※

Have I put my trust in lifeless silver and gold, losing all sense of vitality and humanity?

How can I repay the Lord for all his goodness to me?
Psalm 116:12

During the summer of my seventeenth year, my one goal was to pass my driving test and obtain my license. Having done that, my immediate second goal was to obtain a car. A neighbor of ours frequently bought and sold used cars. He enjoyed cars and did this more for fun than profit. That summer he had come across a bright red, 1963 Dodge Dart, ten years old, mint condition. He wanted four hundred fifty dollars for the car.

I had always held summer jobs but I did not have $450 readily available. I spoke to my grandfather about a short-term loan. I would pay him back in full as soon as I had the money. He agreed. Zero interest. Full repayment. Dodge Dart as collateral. A deal was struck.

Several months later I had collected the money. I drove to Brooklyn to repay my debt. My grandfather was sitting out on his front porch. I approached him, kissed his cheek, and handed him the money. "What's this for?" he questioned. "The money you lent me for the car." "I don't know what you're talking about." "Grandpa, you lent me $450." "Put your money away. Go inside and say hello to Grandma."

I learned a great lesson that day. I caught a glimpse of the Lord's generosity on a front porch in Brooklyn.

The bottom line is the Lord asks only that we love Him. The truth is, in fact, we couldn't even begin to pay Him back.

❖

Lord do I understand that your generosity is unending and without remuneration?

Praise the Lord, all you nations; extol him, all you peoples. For great is his love toward us, and the faithfulness of the Lord endures forever. Praise the Lord.

Psalm 117

Early one Tuesday morning in the summer, I went to Mass at our church. I enjoy the quietness of a weekday service. The congregation is much smaller, the lighting a little dimmer, the service a little more personal.

On this particular morning, there were about fifty or sixty people present in the church. What struck me most was the ecclectic nature of this group of people seeking God at this early hour. There were several men in business suits. They were obviously on their way to work. There were two teenage boys with matching shirts sporting a team logo. They looked as if they were heading for baseball or soccer practice. Several older couples, retirees I guessed, were in attendance. They all wore shorts. A few younger people were in shorts, also. They must have been on vacation. There was a postal worker in his summer uniform.

All of these people, some young, some old, some heading to work, some on vacation, all of them, took the time out at six A.M. to praise the Lord. They all rose early to be with Him, not just privately in their own rooms, but publicly with their spiritual brothers and sisters. Praise the Lord, indeed, all you nations.

❉

Do I sometimes go out of my way to be with the Lord, to share His love even when it is not so convenient to do so?

The stone the builders rejected has become the capstone;
the Lord has done this and it is marvelous in our eyes.

Psalm 118:22

Many years ago a young high school student needed money for school. He began working in a medical laboratory at a major teaching hospital. He was relegated the task of washing the laboratory glassware: beakers, flasks, test tubes. His family did not have tuition money for college. He was not gifted enough for academic or athletic scholarships. His neighbors and friends told him completing high school was good enough. His teachers did not encourage continued studies. Undaunted, he pressed on.

College tuition was a struggle. He continued to wash bottles. Graduating college was a major milestone to his friends and family. Everyone felt he should be satisfied. But he wanted more. He refused to stop. Graduate school was even more expensive. He added cab driver to his resume.

I met him when I was a second-year medical student. He was still working in the lab. Only now, he was the chairman of the department of clinical microbiology. From bottle washer to chairman, that's a long road. He could easily have been the cornerstone the builders cast away, but he refused to be. He was, without question, the capstone of my medical education.

❊

Do I have the strength to ignore other people's
rejection and press on in my endeavors?

How can a young man keep his way pure? By living according to your word. Open my eyes that I may see the wonderful things in your law.

I was having dinner with a third-year law student. We were discussing law school and her future plans. One of the other dinner guests turned the conversation toward a recent contract dilemma he was having.

The outcome of the conversation was that it was important for any contract to have in place a strong working agreement without locking in oneself. The key to a good contract, I was told, was the careful wording of a way out of that contract.

In other words, a loophole. Yes, actually, multiple loopholes. Any good contract should contain, discreetly of course, several bailouts, if need be.

That, it seems, has become the standard operating procedure for law in this country. The law no longer seems to be something to love and behold. It has become a series of evasions and escape routes to get us off the hook.

And we seem to be taking the same approach with God's laws. We look for the loopholes. That wasn't really lusting. I didn't really use God's name in vain. It wasn't actually adultery, or stealing, or lying. Instead of cherishing the Lord's commandments, we're out there negotiating loopholes. No wonder Moses smashed the tablets.

※

Lord, do I find comfort in your commandments?
Do I rejoice in your laws?

I call on the Lord in my distress, and he answers me. Save me, O Lord, from lying lips and from deceitful tongues.

Psalm 120:1–2

It is interesting that I should be reflecting upon this Psalm in the midst of President Clinton's grand jury testimony. What fascinates me most about this whole fiasco is not the alleged sexual encounters, or the abuse of power, or even the total lapse in executive judgment. No, what I find most troubling is the exhaustive pretestimonial planning and scheming.

What should the president say? Should he admit he did it? Did something? Did nothing? Deny it all? Admit it all? Did some things but didn't inhale? The political theorists are in a frenzy speculating the outcome of every possible scenario.

Yet no one has even mentioned, in fact, even hinted, that maybe the man should just tell the truth. After all, shouldn't that be his only option? He is the leader of our country, the leader of the free world, a professed Christian, under judicial oath. Yet his stategists work feverishly formulating a response. Formulating a response.

This sets a poor precedent for our entire nation. If our own leader needs to formulate his answers, what hope is there for any of us? Is this the message we want to send to our children, our allies, ourselves? Americans have always been criticized for being too brutally honest, too brashly outspoken, in the name of truth. We no longer seem to be having this problem.

❖

Lord, am I still able to speak the truth or have I fallen prey to lying lips and a deceitful tongue?

I lift my eyes to the hills—where does my help come from? My help comes from the Lord, the Maker of heaven and earth.

Psalm 121:1–2

There is a practice in sports, baseball in particular, that I haven't decided if I am in favor of or against. It is the practice of players making the sign of the cross when they get up to bat. I've heard comments on both sides of the issue.

Some say it is nothing more than a thoughtless ritual. It's showy. It takes a religious sign and turns it into a superstitious gesture. God is not going to intervene on a batter's behalf. He is not in the business of doctoring fast balls.

On the other hand, though, what if that small gesture symbolizes that player offering his performance to the Lord, or simply asking the Lord for help? I ask the Lord for His help in everything I do, before surgery, before lecturing, in raising my children. Are these requests for His help any more or less noble than the athlete's?

In my mind, if a player, in those few seconds of signing, is saying to the Lord, "please help me here," or simply thinking, "Lord, this is the gift you gave me. Help me use it to the fullest," then I find the gesture refreshing. I believe the Lord is with us in everything we do. Yes, I know He's not calling balls and strikes, but it is nice to know He's in the batter's box with us.

❈

*Do I lift my eyes to you, asking for your help,
in everything I do?*

For the sake of my brothers and friends, I will say, "Peace be with you."

Psalm 122:8

My wife and I were invited to hear an up and coming singer. He was performing at a local coffee house near our home. He played guitar, wrote and sang his own songs. The evening sounded perfect, a relaxing coffee house with new musical talent.

The singer was quite good. Unfortunately, though, there was an aura of anger about him that was almost disturbing to watch. One could see the hostility in his face as he sang. It was almost frightening.

This young performer does not seem to be alone in his anger. When I listen to the words and watch the performances of many of today's young recording artists, they seem to be seething with anger. What is all the hostility about? There seems to be a whole generation of incensed youths out there. Their song lyrics are resentful. Their facial expressions snarling. Their concerts and clubs crammed with mosh pits and body slamming.

There appears to be an obvious absence of inner peace and tranquility among our young. I find that sad. Youth is supposed to carry with it optimism and hope. For a generation thriving on coolness, they seem to be awfully hot under the collar. I wonder if our leftover incense would help?

❄

Lord, do I realize I can turn to You as a
source of inner peace?

Have mercy on us, O Lord, have mercy on us, for we have endured much contempt. We have endured much ridicule from the proud, much contempt from the arrogant.

Psalm 123:3–4

My brother teaches high school English. He didn't always. In fact, he is somewhat new to the field of teaching. He returned to graduate school for his degree in education when he was in his thirties. Prior to that, he was a stock broker.

He was one of the few people I have ever met who left Wall Street during the height of a market surge. In short, he refused to sell his soul for the company for which he was working. He had a hard time pushing clients to buy certain stocks favored by his brokerage house. He had a hard time persuading elderly couples to shift secure funds into high risk ventures. He had a hard time pressuring family and friends.

His coworkers ridiculed him for being too honest. He just didn't have that killer instinct they told him. He could have made a fortune. The proud and the arrogant certainly were.

He left, he told me, when he could no longer tell the difference between suggested buys and stock manipulation. He forfeited a substantial income with that move, but then again it was his face in the mirror each morning.

❖

Am I willing to accept the ridicule of the arrogant for following your ways, Lord?

If the Lord had not been on our side—the flood would have engulfed us, the torrent would have swept over us, the raging waters would have swept us away.

Psalm 124:1, 4–5

The priest who performed our wedding ceremony was made pastor of a parish church just outside Baltimore. We recently had dinner together. During the meal he told us of two young girls in his parish who were killed. One died in an automobile accident, the other the victim of a homicide. Both girls were teenagers; both of their deaths were tragic.

The two families were handling the tragedies very differently. One family appeared to be coping relatively well. They were supportive of each other. They found spiritual comfort in their church community. They increased their parish activities, either as a distraction or as a way of giving back to fellow parishioners who had helped them.

The other family, as my friend told us, had not been very faithful even before tragedy struck. The death of their daughter became an unbearable situation. The family came apart. The father sought comfort in alcohol, barely earning a living. The mother, totally distraught, has been unable to cope with the necessities of daily living.

None of us can predict how we would cope with such tragedy. But how does one even begin to handle such tragedy without faith? What support can there be? What hope? What comfort? Without the Lord's hand, I know I would surely be swept away by such a catastrophe.

✠

How could I even begin to cope with tragedy in my life without the Lord's comfort?

The scepter of the wicked will not remain over the land alotted to the righteous, for then the righteous might use their hands to do evil.

Psalm 125:3

Drug sting operations are not uncommon, especially in large cities such as New York. What was interesting about this recently reported buy and bust operation, though, was the suspect that it yielded. A middle-aged priest from Brooklyn was caught buying crack cocaine. The story was unclear as to whether the drugs were bought solely for personal consumption or were purchased for distribution and resale. It doesn't much matter in the overall scheme of things.

Last year a rabbi, also from Brooklyn, was arrested on similar charges. I don't think these situations are unique to Brooklyn clergy. We hear of similar tragedies in other cities, too. We read about stings netting school teachers, health care professionals, police officers, and public officials.

Those citizens around us who are supposed to protect us, who are supposed to be our pillars of righteousness, have themselves become instruments of evil. Where goodness is supposed to reign, evil prevails.

And do not think for one second that we could not fall prey to the same wickedness. Would Satan gain any greater pleasure than the downfall of the good person? Could he claim any greater victory?

⌘

Do I recognize in myself the potential for evil, my vulnerability for wickedness?

Those who sow in tears will reap with songs of joy. He who goes out weeping, carrying seed to sow, will return with songs of joy, carrying sheaves with him.

Psalm 126:5–6

Of all of the things I have accomplished in my lifetime, medical school was, without question, the most difficult. The work was endless. There were not enough hours in the day to complete the expected tasks. Countless textbooks had to be not just read, but memorized. The concepts of medicine were not nearly as difficult as the enormous volumes of material to be learned. Literally, years were spent memorizing anatomy, physiology, pathology, pharmacology. The burden was sometimes crushing.

But almost in an instant, the painful years of sowing the seeds of medical knowledge gave way to the joys of clinical medicine. Delivering my first baby, tying my first sutures during surgery, setting my first fracture, all brought incredible waves of joy.

In retrospect, the only way those joyful moments could have been made possible were through the painful sowing of those early years. Had I not sown the seeds in medical school, irrespective of how painful they were, I never would have experienced the joyful harvest.

But isn't everything in life like that? Nothing worthwhile can endure, not our marriages, our children, our careers, or our faith, without the pain and weeping in sowing those initial seeds. Only then can we return from the harvest with songs of joy.

⚜

Am I willing to sow in tears to reap the benefit of the joyful harvest?

Unless the Lords builds the house, its builders labor in vain.

Psalm 127:1

One of the more difficult messages we try to convey to our children is that all of our blessings come from the Lord. They believe most of them come from the mall. We ask them to thank God, in their prayers, for our blessings, for all of the good things He has bestowed upon us. We ask them to look around themselves to see how truly fortunate they are.

My wife often asks why have we been permitted such blessings while incredible suffering surrounds us. Why were we born into a country of significant wealth and political stability? Why were we born to parents who worked hard to educate us, to provide for us, to guide us into adulthood? I look around at others living in war-torn nations, states of poverty and famine, families broken and abusive, and I ask why was I spared all of that?

The only answer I can arrive at is that all of my blessing stem from the Lord. My station in life, my attributes, my lineage, my skills are all gifts from the Lord. I did not earn them. I did not achieve them. No amount of toiling or sweat can change that. Sure I can build upon the gifts the Lord has given me. I can work hard to develop and not waste those treasures, but the gifts themselves, those blessings, are His alone to give.

⌖

Lord, do I realize that everything I possess is from you?
You are the builder, I am the house.

Your wife will be like a fruitful vine within your house;
your sons will be like olive shoots around your table.

Psalm 128:3

My brother-in-law is into gardening in a big way. While many of us may have small vegetable patches somewhere in our backyards, Michael has tilled a miniature farm in his. By summer's end, he has produced enough vegetables to supply the entire family with bushels of produce. But he will be the first to tell you that his yield is only as good as the strength of his plants. No mattter how much he waters, cultivates, or nurtures, if his plants are weak, they produce nothing.

The psalmist's analogy of the vine and motherhood is then so appropriate. My children's growth and development can only come about through my wife's strength. She is their lifeline. She nurtures them. She provides their nutrition, physically, spiritually, emotionally. Like Michael's garden, the harvest is only as abundant as the strength of his plants.

Likewise, the growth of our children into loving, caring, giving adults is the direct result of my wife's vine. Her strength, her nutrition, her support, is their lifeline. The most beautiful grapes can only come about from the healthiest vine.

❊

Lord, help me to realize that the growth and
maturation of my children can only come about
through the strength of my vine.

But the Lord is righteous; he has cut me free from the cords of the wicked.

Psalm 129:4

A Klu Klux Klan leader, Sam Bowers, was recently convicted of murder, thirty years after he committed his heinous crime. He apparently led a Klan mob responsible for burning the home of a black grocer, working to achieve black voting rights in the south. On four previous occasions, the murder trials had resulted in deadlocked juries.

What led to a successful conviction this time, was the testimony of a then nineteen-year-old boy that Bowers had befriended. It seems the boy was present at the cafe when Bowers gave his orders to murder the civil rights grocer.

For thirty years, this witness harbored knowledge of the crime. Whether it was fear or misguided loyalty that prevented him from speaking out is unclear. What is clear though, is that thirty years later, the Lord cut him free from the cords of the wicked.

That is never easy to do. The very real possibility of retaliation is always present. We have seen it in gang members who leave, organized crime figures who turn. The snares of the wicked can be all-encompassing and inescapable. It is only with the Lord's help that these cords can be cut and we can be set free.

⚜

Help me to break free from the cords of the wicked and set my life free.

If you, O Lord, kept a record of sins, O Lord, who could stand? But with you there is forgiveness.

Psalm 130:3–4

If the Lord is keeping a running tally of my infractions, then I think I am in significant trouble. I pray, as did the psalmist, that every office supply borrowed, every profanity murmured, every possession desired, is not being recorded. Because if they are, who among us could survive that kind of scrutiny. We know we can ask for the Lord's forgiveness for any of our judgmental lapses, whether they be trivial or serious.

Despite that though, if we believe that we have been created in the image of God, then we must go beyond that. We cannot be content with simply asking the Lord for forgiveness. We, too, have to be willing to forgive those who have sinned against us. We have to be willing to destroy the list, to forgive and forget, to give others a fresh start.

That, of course, is the much harder thing to do. To relish in the Lord's forgiveness means not simply asking for His pardon when we have sinned, but to be willing to turn the other cheek when it is asked of us. Forgiveness comes from God and only by forgiving others can we even begin to see the Lord's presence within ourselves. As St. Francis says, "It is only in pardoning that we are pardoned."

✠

*Lord, you set the example of forgiveness,
help me to follow your lead and forgive
those who trespass against me.*

My heart is not proud, O Lord, my eyes are not haughty:
I do not concern myself with great matters or things too
wonderful for me.

Psalm 131:1

I was recently at a golf outing and fund raising dinner. I was speaking to one of the people connected with the event when another golfer approached us. He was a local politician, a town mayor. The person I was speaking to wanted to introduce me to the mayor. I had seen his name in the paper several times. I was happy to make his aquaintance.

He was, however, one of those people who doesn't look you in the eye when he shakes your hand. He looked right past me to see whose hand he would be shaking next. Not once during the entire twenty or thirty second introduction did he ever make eye contact. He was too busy scanning the crowd behind me for his next contact.

This individual seemed to have little interest in the people at this outing, other than to use the event to promote his own campaign. His concern seemed to be the great matters that were beyond the dinner. He didn't socialize; he worked the room. His eyes never seemed to drift down from their haughty position but rather stayed fixed on those things that would bring him fame and prestige.

❊

Am I too concerned with those things that are
self-serving and arrogant?

I will not enter my house or go to my bed—I will allow no sleep to my eyes, no slumber to my eyelids, till I find a place for the Lord, a dwelling for the Mighty One of Jacob.

Psalm 132:3–5

One weekend during my orthopedic residency, I was on call at our trauma center hospital. We would be on call every third weekend from Saturday morning until we went home Monday evening. Sleep was sporadic and occasional. Trauma centers tend to be busy.

This particular weekend was especially busy. A neighboring hospital had to close its emergency room for boiler repairs. Over the course of the weekend, I saw thirty-four orthopedic patients in the emergency room and admitted seventeen of them for surgery. The work was nonstop. I had no sleep. I was found at five-thirty, Monday morning, asleep at a nursing station. My head was in a patient's chart. I had fallen asleep writing my notes and orders.

Most surgical residencies are like that, five years of work with exceedingly little sleep. In fact, for those years, sleep was all I craved. It was, without question, my most precious commodity. Sleep is a basic necessity for life. Yet the psalmist tells us he was willing to forgo sleep until he found a place for the Lord.

That place he speaks of could be a physical place, or more likely for us, it means a personal place within our lives. Where does the Lord fit into our lives? Are we ever able to rest until we feel secure that He is with us? Can we ever sleep until God is in our lives?

※

Am I at peace knowing that the Lord
is in my life?

How good and pleasant it is when brothers live together in unity.

Psalm 133:1

The classic film *Boys Town* contains one of the most touching and memorable scenes ever recorded. The older brother carried his younger, fallen brother for miles. When asked how he was able to transport such a burdensome load, he replied, "He ain't heavy. He's my brother." The boy's love and concern for his brother's welfare far outweighed his physical mass.

Contrast that with the heinous crime portrayed in Genesis, when Cain murders his own brother, Abel. What makes that crime so horrific is that it occurred between two brothers. Abel's murder sets the backdrop for a basic question asked within the first few chapters of the Bible, "Am I my brother's keeper?"

The entire remainder of the Bible goes on to answer that question with a resounding, yes. We are, indeed, our brother's keeper. We are responsible for his well being. We are responsible for his care. We should not hesitate to carry his load, to feel his pain, to comfort his suffering.

✠

Do I live by the credo, "I am my brother's keeper"?

Praise the Lord, all you servants of the Lord who minister by night in the house of the Lord.

Psalm 134:1

There is a syndrome in medicine called sundowning. It frequently occurs in hospitalized, elderly patients. During the late night hours, they often become confused and disoriented. It is most likely due to a combination of pain medications, unfamiliar surroundings, and early dementia. The experience can be quite frightening to these frail patients.

Our nurses are trained to recognize and treat sundowning quickly. The crux of this treatment is reassurance. Patients need to be comforted and reassured that the new surroundings are safe. They need to know that no one is trying to harm them.

I am sure our spiritual lives are no different. There are times when we go through periods of darkness and uncertainty. Times when we become disoriented, confused and frightened. The environment is new; the way is unclear. It is during these times that we, too, need reassurance. We need the guidance of someone to tell us it's O.K., that we are not lost. We are safe in these new surroundings. We need these ministers of the night, these spiritual nurses, to guide us through our own personal sundowns.

※

Am I able to see my way through those periods of spiritual darkness in my life, times when I feel alone and frightened?

The idols of the nations are silver and gold, made by the hand of men.

Psalm 135:15

I often see patients in my office who are originally from Europe, Asia, or South America. They are now living in the United States. Many have been transferred here on business. Some have relocated here on a semi-permanent basis. I always ask them how they enjoy living in the States. The vast majority love it here. Interestingly, though, most have the same criticism of our country. Namely, that we as a nation are too preoccupied with money.

Money is everything here and everything we do is money oriented. They feel that we place too great an emphasis on earning money and keeping money. We work too hard for it. We rarely enjoy what we have. We are always striving for more. Sadly, we seem to have lost our ability to enjoy life without it. We tend to neglect family, friends, and even ourselves in an effort to earn a few more dollars.

How sad. We have established idols of gold and silver, and we are running ourselves ragged trying to serve these idols. How many latch-key children have raised themselves because both parents are working to give them a "better" life? How many marriages breakup because one or both partners have made their career their devoted spouse? If that is what we worship, then we have only ourselves to blame when we end up alone and empty.

※

Have I forsaken my friends and family in serving the gods of gold and silver?

Give thanks to the Lord of Lords: to the one who re-
membered us in our low estate and freed us from our en-
emies.

Psalm 136:3, 23–24

The insightful comic strip Pogo once proclaimed, "I have seen the enemy, and it is us." How true. We are, without question, our own worst enemies. We are filled with self-doubt, anxiety, and senseless fears. We lose confidence in ourselves. We talk ourselves out of things we should have the confidence to do. We convince ourselves to do things that get us into all sorts of trouble.

We eat too much. We get depressed. We drink too much. We spend too much money. We spend too little time. We alone bring these maladies upon ourselves.

So when we ask the Lord to save us from our enemies, of whom do we speak? Most often, I suppose, we need to be saved from ourselves. The enemy is not out there. It is right here. It is us.

If that is the case, then the enemy will always be with us. The best we can hope for is that with the Lord's help, we can be protected from ourselves. We will always have our shortcomings, our evils, our vices. Hopefully, with the Lord's help, we can acknowledge them and minimize their control over our lives. Otherwise, we remain at their mercy. We remain in their grasp.

✠

Can I come to grips with my own shortcomings
and realize that the problem is often not out there
but right here within myself?

*May my tongue cling to the roof of my mouth if I do not
remember you.*

Psalm 137:6

Several years ago we spent a long holiday weekend in
Washington, D.C. My oldest daughter's class was
studying the White House and our government. She
was anxious to visit the city. We thought it would be a
nice trip for the whole family.

As typical tourists to our nation's capitol, we visited
the usual agenda of sites, the White House, the Washington, Lincoln, and Jefferson Memorials, the Air and
Space Museum. The kids' interest level on any given
day was a direct inverse of their fatigue level.

We stopped to see the Vietnam Memorial, The
Wall. For anyone who has not seen the memorial, it is a
series of simple black granite slabs standing vertically.
The names of all of those killed during the conflict are
engraved onto its face. No fancy towers, columns, statues, or vaults, just a simple wall of names.

Yet, my kids were more attentive there than at any
other time during our stay. They quietly walked the
wall and said nothing. They scanned each row of
names. I could see on their faces a seriousness that was
not present before.

My middle daughter was on my shoulders as we
walked. She asked, "Dad, what are all these names?" I
explained. Her only reply, "What a waste, Dad."
"From the mouth of babes," I thought to myself.

It is important that we remember. It is important

that we do not forget our heroes, our fallen, our forefathers, and our creator. To all of them, we owe our lives.

❦

*Do I take the time to remember all of those
who have gone before me, who have shaped my life,
both physically and spiritually?*

Though I walk in the midst of trouble, you preserve my life; you stretch your hand against the anger of my foes, with your right hand you save me.

Psalm 138:7

A friend of mine is a priest. We were having dinner when he told us about a woman in his parish. Her daughter had been killed in a car accident several months earlier. The mother was devastated by the loss and was having a difficult time coping. She prayed her daughter was safe. My friend wanted to help her but was limited in what he could do.

Then one day she met with him and she appeared drastically changed. Her spirits had returned. She told my friend that she had dreamt about her daughter. She saw her in her dream. The girl was happy. She was safe. She told her mother not to worry about her. In the dream, the mother noticed that the girl was limping. She told her mother that she had hurt her leg but she was fine.

When the mother awoke, she felt reassured but she realized that she had never spoken to the coroner after her daughter's death. She met with the coroner and spoke to him about his findings. Her daughter had apparently died of internal injuries. Other than that, there had been no other serious injuries, except for a broken ankle.

The mother left in silence. In her dream, she had seen her daughter limping and now for the first time, discovered that she had had an ankle fracture. The mother was reassured that her daughter was indeed safe. In the midst of her troubles, the Lord had reached out to her and allowed her a glimpse into heaven.

※

Do I have the courage to take the Lord's hand when He reaches out to me in times of trouble?

For you created my inmost being; you knit me together in my mother's womb.

Psalm 139:13

My wife had an appointment one morning with the dentist. She had not had a full dental X-ray series for several years. The dentist recommended the series. Numerous X-rays were taken from every conceivable angle, front, side, top, panoramic, aerial views, the whole works. Her teeth were fine. Later that day she realized that she was late with her period. Not wasting any time, she purchased a home pregnancy test.

Much to our surprise, the test was positive. Now my wife was in a panic. Not because she was pregnant, but because she thought she may have done some harm to the baby with her battery of radiographs. She had me call every dentist and radiologist on staff at the hospital. All of them reassured her that the baby should be fine. Still, for nine months we worried. Thankfully, Nicole was born unharmed.

In my mind, the womb is a sacred place, as sacred as any church sanctuary or tabernacle. It is the place where the Lord begins and completes the miracle of life. For any of you who have witnessed the process, you know that it is truly miraculous. The entire concept of the creation of life within another being is mind-boggling. If our bodies are temples of the Lord, then this must indeed be the holiest of holy places. For it is here that the Lord breathes into us the spirit of life and it is here that we come to know the Father.

❖

Can I appreciate how truly miraculous
the creation of life is?

Do not grant the wicked their desires, O Lord; do not let their plans succeed, or they will become proud. Let the heads of those who surround me be covered with the trouble their lips have caused. Let burning coals fall upon them; may they be thrown into the fire, into miry pits, never to rise.

Psalm 140:8–10

I witnessed true wickedness today. There was a news program on television about child pornographers and pedophiles. A very young looking, undercover news reporter was assisting police and federal agents in capturing these offenders. She was posing as a fourteen-year-old girl in internet chat rooms. She said that within seconds of her signing on, she would be swarmed with scores of pedophiles responding to her screen name. Many tried to entice her into meeting with them. Most sent her pornographic material via her computer.

On multiple occasions, the police used her to draw these pedophiles into situations where they could be arrested. Many were. They came from all walks of life, from blue-collar workers to white-collar professionals. Quite honestly, most were indistinguishable from any of our neighbors.

At their arrests, most were arrogant. They had gotten away with their crimes for so long, they thought they were invincible. One man wanted his money refunded for the plane tickets he sent to the young girl.

These are the wicked who prey on our young. They

have become ruthless and proud. May they indeed be tortured and thrown into the fire. May their wicked plans and desires never succeed.

※

Do I have the strength to intervene and stop wickedness when I see it?

Set a guard over my mouth, O Lord; keep watch over the door of my lips.

Ps. 141:3

On several occasions throughout my married life, I have received the infamous kick under the table from my wife. On days when I am at my best, I understand the gesture to mean, "Stop saying whatever it is I am saying." On more typical days, when I am not paying particular attention, I will reflexly respond, "What?" This is often followed by an even more vigorous kick. Hopefully, by that time, I will have gotten the message.

Women, in general, seem to be much better communicators than men. I think they are more practiced at it. They tend to be more adept at conveying their feelings and more importantly, at reading other people's. They are more atuned to the sentiments of others. They grasp more quickly the real meaning of what others are trying to say.

Men can often be oblivious to that. We tend to communicate solely for the purpose of conveying a course of action or cheering on a sports team. Sentiment is often secondary. Hence, the kick under the table. I understand well the psalmist's plea for the Lord to guard his lips. I guesss his legs were killing him.

❄

Do I understand that my words can inflict pain and suffering just as easily as they can comfort and reassure?

Look to my right and see; no one is concerned for me. I have no refuge; no one cares for my life.

Psalm 142:4

Several years ago a friend of ours committed suicide. She was being treated for depression. According to her family, she was overcome with guilt, hopelessness, and despair. When a new business venture failed, she felt she had become a burden to her family. Despite encouragement from family and friends, her plight must have appeared hopeless to her. She must have felt that the only way out of her situation was to end her life.

What is sad is that those who truly cared for her were unable to help. Even with a supportive family around her, she felt as if she had no one to her right or to her left. Although they cared deeply for her, she considered herself a burden to them. Sadly, I am sure their greatest burden came after her death. How does one even begin to cope with the self-inflicted death of wife, mother, friend?

I am sure the Lord was with her always but in the midst of her troubles, she may have lost sight of that. Hopefully, her family and friends never will.

⚜

When everything seems hopeless, when I feel that no one is concerned for me, do I know that I can turn to the Lord to rescue me?

*Teach me to do your will, for you are my God; may your
good spirit lead me on level ground.*

Psalm 143:10

One of the nice things about having kids in school is
that I get a chance to repeat all of those courses I have
already taken in school. By helping with homework
and test reviews, I have again become proficient in
fifth-grade math, second-grade spelling, and eighth-
grade social studies. I am also learning Italian, perfect-
ing my multiplication, and developing an entirely new
outlook on capital letters.

I recently had the chance to begin teaching my
youngest daughter the Lord's prayer. It is enjoyable because it allows me to explain each line to her as we go
along. "Art in heaven" and "hallowed be thy name" always draw looks of puzzlement from young students.
But "thy will be done" offers me a chance to explain to
her that our desires, our wishes, are secondary to the
Lord's.

We have to ask ourselves, what is the Lord asking us
to do? What does He really expect from us? Does He
demand more from some than from others? How do I
know what the Lord is asking of me?

That's a lot for a seven-year-old to grasp. It's a lot for
any of us. It's only by reading the Lord's word, though,
by opening our hearts to the spirit, that we can even
begin to learn His will. Let's hope the social studies is a
little easier to explain.

✠

*Do I allow myself the time to understand
what the Lord is asking of me?*

Deliver me and rescue me from the hands of foreigners whose mouths are full of lies, whose right hands are deceitful. Then our sons in their youth will be like well nurtured plants, and our daughters will be like pillars carved to adorn a palace. Our barns will be filled with every kind of provision. Our sheep will increase by thousands.

Psalm 144:11–13

Hardly a week passes that we do not read about some crime committed against recent immigrants to our nation. From small towns to large cities, foreigners are assaulted, robbed, persecuted and tormented. The reasons for such acts are as numerous as the attacks themselves.

Immigrants are easy targets. Their command of the language may be poor. Many of them fear legal prosecution or even deportation. They are often blamed for job losses and economic strife. Many are attacked simply because they are different. Xenophobia, fear of foreigners, is pervasive throughout our society.

Unfortunately, many people feel that their economic woes are due solely to the presence of foreigners. Their lives would be better, their coffers overflowing, their garages filled, but for these strangers in our land.

Is that really the case, though, or are we simply afraid of those who may be different from us? Do we mistrust what we don't know? Do we blame the easy target instead of looking for the harder truth? The psalmist certainly did. Are we harboring those very same sentiments?

❉

Do I take the time to understand those who may be different from me?

All you have made will praise you, O Lord; your saints will extol you. They will tell of the glory of your kingdom and speak of your might, so that all men will know of your mighty acts and the glorious splendor of your kingdom.

Psalm 145:10–12

There is a story about St. Therese of Lisieux, the Little Flower. While she was traveling, her cart became trapped in the mud during a rainstorm. She struggled unsuccessfully to free the vehicle. In the midst of her plight, she looked skyward and proclaimed, "If this is how you treat your friends, no wonder you have so few of them."

St. Paul, one of the most prolific and insightful scriptural writers, spent years of his life persecuting the early Christians. He was a proclaimed enemy of the Jesus of Nazareth. St. Francis, in his youth, was a womanizing, wealthy, party boy. St. Matthew was a tax collector, despised by many of his fellow citizens.

These are our saints. Many were not very saintly. Most were not born sporting halos. But that is, in fact, the very essence of sainthood, overcoming the human condition to extol the glory of God. It is in that very act, of going beyond one's own frailties, that we can gain inspiration. Despite their faults, their shortcomings, their deficiencies, these individuals dedicated their lives to proclaiming the splendor of God's kingdom so that we may come to know Him.

❈

Can I get past my own shortcomings
to proclaim the glory of God's kingdom,
the splendor of His works?

Do not put your trust in princes, in mortal men who cannot save. When their spirit departs, they return to the ground; on that very day their plans come to nothing.

Psalm 146:3–4

So in which prince do we put our trust? Is it the political prince, the leaders of our nations, only to have our trust shattered when they act irresponsibly or selfishly? Or is it the athletic prince? Do we then become dismayed as we watch them succumb to drugs and other vices that the excesses of wealth can bring?

Or is it the financial prince, riding high until his portfolios collapse or he is caught misappropriating funds? Or could it be the religious prince, who may put secular desires ahead of the Lord's plans, resulting in his tearful confessions and televised apologies?

The problem arises when we elevate these individuals to godly heights, when we place them on lofty pedestals from which they can only fall. We are all imperfect beings. We all design imperfect plans. We are all indeed mere mortals whose plans return to nothing.

Our faith then, should be only in the Lord. He alone can succeed to infinity. He alone can guide us. He alone can carry us to safety when our failing spirit grounds us. Only the Lord alone can bring our plans to fruition.

❈

Do I put my faith in the plans of people only to have them dashed by human frailties?

His pleasure is not in the strength of the horse, nor his delight in the legs of a man; the Lord delights in those who fear him, who put their hope in his unfailing love.

Psalm 147:10–11

Several years ago, at the Olympic Games in Barcelona, an image captured my attention and remained permanently etched in my memory. Derek Redman, a sprinter from England, tore his hamstring muscle during his Olympic medal race. There were no warning signs, no collision with another sprinter. The muscle simply tore in mid-race.

Despite his severe pain, Redman was determined to finish the race. Clutching his thigh, he began limping the remaining distance. As he rounded the turn of the track, his father lept from the stands and ran to his son's side. With his father's support, Derek crossed the finish line and collapsed in pain.

I doubt anyone remembers who won that particular race. The fastest time, the strongest legs were long forgotten. What was memorable, though, was the humbled sprinter reaching out to his father for support. What will never be forgotten is the father leaping to his son's aide without hesitation, without being asked.

Is it any different with us? Does the Lord truly care who among us is the strongest, the fastest, the richest? Those qualities that we hold in such high regard, that we use as bragging rights, have little place in the Lord's kingdom. He simply asks that we love Him. For in doing so, He will undoubtedly leap from the stands to save us.

✠

Can I simply put my faith in the Lord's unfailing love without boasting about my attributes?

*Let them praise the name of the Lord, for he commanded
and they were created.*

Psalm 148:5

My daughter asked me what was the point of mos-
quitoes. Her exact words, as she angrily scratched a recent bite, were, "Dad, what do we need them for?"
Unfortunately, during her time of pronounced itching,
no simple answer would suffice. Only the complete annihilation of the entire species would have satisfied her.

On a more philosophical level, though, who are we
to question God's creations? Should creatures exist
only to serve our needs? To many lawn owners, the
lowly dandelion is nothing more than a pesty weed. Yet
upon closer inspection, it sports a beautiful yellow
flower, sprouts tasty serrated leaves, and has a wispy
seed tuft that children have blown for eons.

Even that nasty mosquito is an engineering work of
art. It flies silently, has a heat-seeking guidance system,
and uses a nasal suction wand to draw its nutrients
from unsuspecting daughters. We may not like all of
the Lord's creations but we have to marvel at them. We
may be blind to their purpose but we still must praise
their creator.

✠

Can I respect all of the Lord's creations,
even those I do not understand?

*Let them praise his name with dancing and make music
to him with tambourine and harp.*

Psalm 149:3

If you haven't seen Whoopi Goldberg's movie *Sister Act*, I would strongly recommend a trip to your local video store. In the film, Whoopi plays a second-rate nightclub singer who witnesses a mob related murder. The police decide to hide her in an inner city parish convent until the trial date.

Despite multiple clashes with the Mother Superior, Whoopi is able to blend her nightclub style of music with the convent's choir music. The result brings fame and notoriety to this impoverished parish. At one point in the film, the previously empty church begins to fill with parishioners drawn in by the music. The monsignor exclaims, "Oh, that music. Did you see the people come in? It calls to them."

Indeed, it should. From Gregorian chant to southern Gospel, from the Ave Maria to Kumbaya, our music is our gift to the Lord. It opens our hearts to Him. It carries our love for Him to the heavens on voices sung high. It is the joy in our hearts released. It is His spirit, within us, set free. So bang, strum and sing that joyful noise to Him.

❈

*Do I let my spirit run free to praise the Lord
with dance and song?*

Let everything that has breath praise the Lord.

Psalm 150:6

Several years ago, I began writing my thoughts on the Psalms. They were really for my own personal enjoyment, just some simple thoughts on verses that struck a chord with me. People read them. Many liked them. They encouraged me to write more. I guess some of my thoughts struck a chord with them also.

There were times when I did not know where the insights came from. There were times when I sat and stared at the verses with nothing to say. Yet always, without fail, the words came. I had my Psalms, my pencil (yes, they were written by hand) and my life experiences, but the Lord provided the ideas. Many times throughout the writing of this book, I truly felt I was merely the instrument for the Lord to do His writing.

When I had one final reflection to write, I looked at this Psalm and smiled. Throughout these reflections, I have tried to show that the Lord is with us in everything we do. Spirituality is not out there somewhere. It is right here, right here in the daily chaos, in the kid's homework, in the work place grind. It is right here in how we relate to our family, our friends, our coworkers, and even our enemies.

I searched for a way to convey that sentiment in one last meaningful sentence and then I saw the psalmist's closing verse and I smiled. Let everything that has breath praise the Lord. Indeed.

✠

HUMCA   242
               .5
               C246

CAPOZZI, JAMES D.
    BESIDE QUIET WATERS :
REFLECTIONS ON THE
PSALMS IN OUR   PAPER

HUMCA   242
               .5
               C246

HOUSTON PUBLIC LIBRARY
CENTRAL LIBRARY

6/13

FEB 00